On Tour

Debrett's New Season

On Tour: Debrett's New Season
Published by Debrett's Limited
18–20 Hill Rise, Richmond,
Surrey TW10 6UA
United Kingdom

WRITER & RESEARCHER: Rhonda Carrier

HEAD OF PUBLISHING: Elizabeth Wyse
SENIOR MANAGING EDITOR: Jo Bryant
ASSISTANT EDITOR: Sarah Corney

DESIGN & ART DIRECTION: pentacorbig, High Wycombe
PROOFREADING & INDEXING: Ruth Massey

ISBN 978–1–870520–76–8

Printed and bound by Oriental Press, Dubai

Visit Debrett's at www.debretts.co.uk
Visit Mercedes-Benz at www.mercedes-benz.co.uk

On Tour

Debrett's New Season

from Glyndebourne to Glastonbury

Contents

Spring

Summer

Autumn

Winter

Drives

The New Season

The origins of the social season, which dates back to the 18th century, were firmly anchored in the marriage market for the upper echelons of society. Well-bred girls were launched into society at the age of 17 or 18 with a formal introduction to the monarch, followed by a whirlwind six months of parties, dances and special events. Gradually these events – which ranged from regattas to flower shows, balls, concerts and horse racing – became milestones in the British social calendar, a socially circumscribed ritual that changed very little until the end of the 20th century.

British society has now moved on from the old social certainties. Codified behaviour has, with very few exceptions, been replaced by spontaneity, and there is now immense social fluidity. A democratic and eclectic appetite for communal enjoyment has supplanted the traditional, rigid barriers of class, age and gender. Since the late 18th century Debrett's has enjoyed a role as the authoritative arbiter of social mores: it is, therefore, uniquely well-qualified to redefine the social season for the 21st century, constructing a calendar of events that reflects both historic tradition and contemporary taste.

What better symbol for the dynamic social setting of the 21st century than Mercedes-Benz? Their luxurious and aspirational motor cars have become synonymous with the adventurous, well-travelled lifestyle that is illustrated in the following pages. They have helped us to break down the barriers of geography and distance, and opened up new horizons. The New Season is no longer a purely English phenomenon, although it embraces many of England's most cherished traditions. It now spans Europe, sampling the best the continent can offer. With each new year, the social calendar reveals an unparalleled vista of activities, places to go, landscapes to explore. It's an ever-changing, ever-inviting, open road.

The days are getting longer, and the first scent of spring is in the air. As bulbs emerge from the frozen winter earth, a range of garden festivals display a profusion of inspirational flowers. Towns and cities are waking from their winter hibernation with an array of music, theatre and literature. Sporting adrenalin is rising, with the visceral excitement of the Grand National and the more elegant thrill of the Boat Race. Venture to the continent and enjoy the verdant landscapes and balmy spring days as you drive past ancient châteaux and medieval cities.

Spring

"It's spring fever. That is what the name of it is. And when you've got it, you want – oh, you don't quite know what it is you do want, but it just fairly makes your heart ache, you want it so!"

Mark Twain

Geneva Automobile Show

March sees eleven days of motoring heaven
as Geneva hosts its world-class car show.

From unabashed luxury to miniature electric city cars, Geneva's International Automobile Show, held at the Swiss city's Palexpo, has something for all car enthusiasts. The four main halls are filled with stands representing the globe's major car manufacturers and many smaller ones. 2008 saw Mercedes-Benz present the new generations of CLS-Class, SLK-Class and SL-Class, plus the new addition to the coupé range, the CLC-Class. As well as standard road cars, there are all-terrain cars, alternative-powered cars, racing cars, 'fun cars' (Quads and the like), as well as accessories, including state-of-the-art navigation systems. Many of the exhibits receive their world premières at the show.

STAY & EAT:
A wide choice of eateries at the venue includes three 'gastronomic' restaurants.
   The Four Seasons Hôtel des Bergues was the city's first hotel and retains a historic ambience alongside its modern luxuries. Its restaurant serves northern Italian fare. www.fourseasons.com/geneva

Explore: *lakeside drive*

It's less than 100 km (65 miles) from Geneva to Lausanne,
via some lovely towns and villages dotted along the shoreline.

GENEVA
- Your starting point.

COPPET
- This picturesque town lies in the shadow of an impressive castle built more than four centuries ago on the site of a 13th-century fortification.

NYONS
- An important Roman town, Nyons still bears testament to the Romans' presence, with artefacts on display in several museums. Its castle was constructed in the 12th century.

MORGES
- Morges also has a castle, built in the 13th century and now home to a museum of military apparel and weaponry, but the town is best known for its wine production.

LAUSANNE
- This vibrant city is blessed with ornate old mansions, beautiful woods and parks, and a buzzing cultural life that includes many festivals and events.
  Just beyond Lausanne, at Lavaux (also famous for its vineyards), L'Auberge du Raisin is a culinary hotspot in a 15th-century house. www.aubergeduraisin.ch

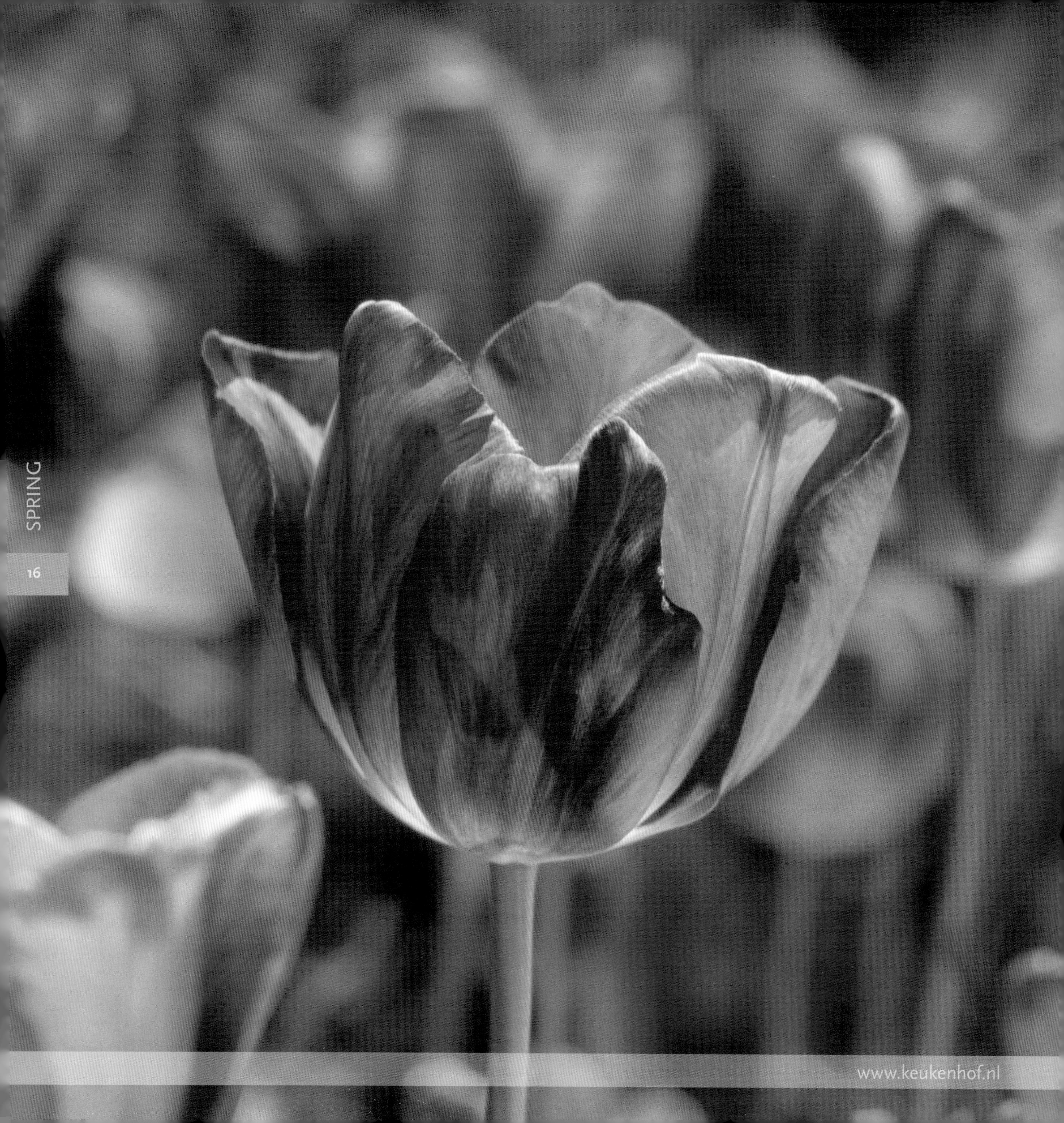

Keukenhof Spring Gardens

Featuring millions of tulips and other bulbs, floral shows and the Netherlands' largest sculpture park within a former castle estate, Keukenhof is one of the season's must-sees. Some of the most impressive Low Country cities are just a short drive away.

Blink and you'll miss it: the world's largest flower garden opens to the public only in spring (March–mid-May), when its famous tulips and other bulb flowers are in full bloom. The idyllic 80-hectare site is also home to three pavilions hosting weekly-changing flower shows, seven themed 'inspiration gardens' displaying the latest garden trends – appealing to both traditional and modern tastes – and around 25 bronze statues by prominent artists. Special events include the passing of the Flower Parade as it makes its way between Noordwijk and Haarlem (April), and bird-of-prey demonstrations.

Drive: *city chic*

This city tour from Lisse, site of the Keukenhof Gardens, to Antwerp, can be enjoyed over a weekend.

THE HAGUE (DEN HAAG)
○ Visit the Mauritshuis, full of Dutch masters such as Vermeer; the Escher Museum devoted to the graphical artist M.C. Escher; and the Gemeentemuseum for works by Dutch artist Piet Mondrian.
www.mauritshuis.nl;
www.escherinhetpaleis.nl;
www.gemeentemuseum.nl

ROTTERDAM
○ Europe's largest port is a former European Capital of Culture. Don't miss the Kunsthal Rotterdam in the Museumpark: 3,300 square metres of striking space, featuring up to 25 exhibitions a year. It was designed by the Dutch architect Rem Koolhaas.
www.kunsthal.nl

ANTWERP
○ This Belgian city is a fashionista's dream, with outlets featuring collections by the likes of Diane von Furstenberg and Dries Van Noten. Many stores are set in and around Nationalestraat; visit the fashion museum, ModeMuseum, also known as MoMu.
www.momu.be

The Boat Race

The annual watery battle between two of Britain's most illustrious universities draws up to a quarter of a million spectators to the banks of the Thames for thrilling views of the tense action. Toasts are raised in the convivial atmosphere of many welcoming riverside pubs.

The world's most famous rowing race began in 1829, when Cambridge student Charles Merivale sent a challenge to his former Harrow schoolfriend Charles Wordsworth (nephew of the poet) at Oxford. Today, tradition holds that the losing team each year issues a challenge to the winner for a re-match the following March or April.

The closest finish in the race's history was in 2003, when there was just a foot between the Cambridge boat and the winners, Oxford. A dead heat was recorded in 1877, but the gap between the boats was thought to be as much as 2 metres (6 ft) – there was no finishing line photography in those days.

The 6.5-km (4.25-mile) race starts out at Putney and finishes at Mortlake; it can be watched all along the course from both sides of the river, but prime viewing spots are: Putney Bridge, Putney Embankment and the towpath in front of Bishops Park at the start; Hammersmith and Barnes towards the middle of the course; and Duke's Meadows and Chiswick Bridge at the end.

STAY

The Bingham: this elegant, boutique-style retreat in a Georgian townhouse in Richmond, close to Mortlake, offers Thames views from its restaurant (especially the gorgeous terrace) and many of its contemporary-styled rooms. www.thebingham.co.uk

EAT

Riva: this outstanding Italian in Barnes, towards the Mortlake end of the boat-race course, offers simple but top-notch dishes from the country's north-eastern region, including wonderful seafood, plus an exemplary wine list. 020 8748 0434

"When one rows it is not the rowing which moves the ship: rowing is only a magical ceremony by means of which one compels a demon to move the ship."

Friedrich Nietzsche

Shakespeare Season

A faithful reconstruction of the Globe open-air amphitheatre on the south bank of the Thames plays host to an inspiring season in which international artists explore the work of the Bard as well as modern-day playwrights.

www.shakespeares-globe.org

> "Shakespeare –
> the nearest thing
> in incarnation to
> the eye of God."
>
> Laurence Olivier

SHAKESPEARE'S GLOBE

This unique venue, which opened in 1997, represents a labour of love by American actor and director Sam Wanamaker, who wanted to commemorate the fact that Shakespeare worked in the Bankside area of London, as the resident playwright for The Lord Chamberlain's Men, who were based in the original Globe Theatre. The result is a painstaking replica of the 17th-century open-air theatre, complete with thatched roof. There's a permanent exhibition here, but the real interest is undoubtedly the theatre season (April–October), when world-class performers interpret several works by Shakespeare as well as new plays.

Ticket prices range from around £15 to £35 for covered seating, or there are cheaper standing tickets; shows continue regardless of rain and last two to three hours. Many spectators opt to stand in the yard since they can move around at will to get the best views. The venue has its own bar and brasserie.

SHAKESPEARE AROUND THE COUNTRY

Regent's Park

This open-air theatre in London's Regent's Park (June–September) is a magical setting for a programme of three of Shakespeare's plays, as well as a classic musical. There's a lawn for picnics, or spectators can pre-book tea and cake or an evening supper.
www.openairtheatre.org

Poole Harbour

The lovely island of Brownsea in Poole Harbour is owned by the National Trust and accessible only by boat. Every year, in July and August, this peaceful outcrop of woodland, heath and marsh is the setting for an open-air staging of one of Shakespeare's works. Spectators can picnic before the show, while the return ferry ride under the stars forms the perfect finale to the whole experience.
www.brownsea-theatre.co.uk

Stratford-upon-Avon

Shakespeare's birthplace has hosted its most illustrious son's plays since the 18th century and is the main home of the Royal Shakespeare Company, which currently plays year-round in the temporary Courtyard Theatre while the Royal Shakespeare Theatre is reconstructed. A new thrust-stage auditorium will reduce the distance between the actors and the audience.
www.rsc.org.uk

STAY

Boasting an impressive lobby bar and elegant restaurant, One Aldwych offers restrained, contemporary glamour just moments from both the river and Covent Garden. Underwater music plays in the swimming pool, and there's a luxurious screening room showing classic movies.
www.onealdwych.com

EAT

Tate Modern Restaurant: awe-inspiring views over the river, St Paul's Cathedral and the City are just part of the attraction of this eatery on the 7th floor of London's powerhouse of modern and contemporary art. Dishes are based on seasonal produce from Britain, Spain and Italy.
www.tate.org.uk

The Grand National

A highlight of the sporting year, this prestigious steeplechase attracts a worldwide television audience of over 600 million viewers, but its dramatic fences and thrilling finishes are best seen in the flesh.

First run in 1839, this world-renowned 7.5-km (4.5-mile) marathon is one of the very few major sports events in which amateurs – both jockeys and trainers – can take on professionals. It takes place in April at Liverpool's Aintree, where riders face 30 of the most challenging fences in jump racing, including The Chair and the notorious Becher's Brook. The latter, named after a rider who fell into its ditch in 1839, features a steep drop followed by a left-hand turn, and is the most testing fence of any horse race.

Arrive early to walk the course, a circuit taking about an hour. The best race views are to be had from the very limited West Tip seats in the recently improved Tattersalls Enclosure with its new Aintree Pavilion – from this area spectators can see The Chair, as well as the parade ring and winner's enclosure, and enjoy access to a private bar.

"It were not best that we should all think alike; it is difference of opinion that makes horse races."

Mark Twain

A WEEKEND IN LIVERPOOL
Twenty years old in 2008, the Tate Liverpool, in a converted warehouse in the revitalised Albert Dock complex, displays modern and contemporary artworks from the mighty Tate Collection, and hosts a changing roster of temporary exhibitions. www.tate.org.uk

Hope Street Hotel is the most desirable accommodation in the city, a luxurious boutique hotel with contemporary interiors within an impressive 19th-century building styled as a Venetian palazzo. The London Carriage Works, Hope Street Hotel's restaurant, is a fashionable spot and offers global modern fare based on seasonal – and often organic – produce. www.hopestreethotel.co.uk

Maltings Beer Festival

One of the few beer festivals to be set in a brewery, Maltings attracts thousands of beer and real ale lovers to try out more than 100 delicious local brews.

This three-day festival, held in Newton Abbot in Devon in mid- to late April, is hosted in one of only six Victorian malthouses to have survived in this country – the art of producing malt from barley is gradually dying out. The low admission price (about £3) includes a half-pint glass for tasting the offerings from around 35 breweries in the West Country and Guernsey.

STAY

Not far from Newton Abbot in Dartmoor National Park, Bovey Castle offers luxurious rooms inside the castle itself or granite lodges within its landscaped gardens. There are indoor and outdoor pools, a spa and an array of activities, including clay shooting and horse-riding. www.boveycastle.com

OTHER BEER FESTIVALS

Local branches of the Campaign for Real Ale organise a huge number of beer festivals throughout the year. CAMRA produces an indispensable annual calendar. www.camra.org.uk

The Cambridge Beer Festival

Britain's oldest beer festival, and the largest outside London, attracts more than 32,000 people over six days in May. It gives festival-goers the chance to sample more than 170 real ales and 60 foreign beers, ciders, English wines and mead. There's also a variety of food stalls, including a very popular cheese counter. www.cambridgebeerfestival.com

The Kent Beer Festival

This three-day event is held in Canterbury in July. It features more than 120 real ales, plus a cider and a foreign beers bar. Food and live music are also on offer. www.kentbeerfestival.co.uk

The Great British Beer Festival

The country's biggest beer festival, held over five days at London's Earl's Court in August, celebrated its 30th anniversary in 2007. It showcases about 450 British and 200 foreign beers, as well as traditional British cider and perry. www.camra.org.uk

The National Winter Ales Festival

Its sister event takes place in Manchester each January, promoting a selection of over 200 beers, including winter ales (such as

> "Beer is proof
> that God loves
> us and wants us
> to be happy."
>
> Benjamin Franklin

stouts and porters) not available at the time of the London festival. Live music acts provide entertainment in the evenings. www.alefestival.org.uk

The Scottish Traditional Beer Festival
This beer fest is held over three days in Edinburgh in June. Visitors can try Schilling Ales – darker, sweeter and less heavily hopped beers unique to Scotland – as well as cider and perry, and bottled beers from Germany. www.camra.org.uk

International
Garden Festival
Chaumont-sur-Loire

A magnificent château and its park overlooking the scenic
Loire is the setting for a long festival celebrating the very
best in contemporary garden design.

Although Chaumont's castle and grounds are open year-round, the prime time to visit is between May and October, when the site hosts its world-renowned festival of contemporary garden design.

Twenty-six plots divided by beech hedges are given over to creations that have been chosen from among several hundred entries from around the world. Some are playful, others elegant and restrained; all are inspiring. That also goes for the gastronomic treats offered in the temporary restaurants set up for the duration of the Festival.

Chaumont's small but classically beautiful castle was occupied by, among others, Catherine de Medici (who entertained Nostradamus there), Diane de Poitiers and Madame de Staël. It has stunning interiors from various epochs and superb Belle Epoque stables boasting porcelain troughs.

The charming village of Chaumont nestles at the foot of the castle on the banks of the Loire, an ideal place for riverside walks.

"How fair is a garden amid the
trials and passions of existence."

Benjamin Disraeli

Explore: *Loire châteaux tour*

VALLEY OF A THOUSAND CHATEAUX

o The Loire Valley and its world-famous châteaux is a UNESCO
World Heritage site; an interesting driving tour might begin at
Chartres and end at Bourges, both also World Heritage sites by
virtue of their cathedrals. Castles to visit *en route* are Châteaudun,
Chambord, Chaumont-sur-Loire, Amboise and Chenonceaux.
Although as a straight run the drive takes about five hours, the
itinerary is best spread over a leisurely three days.

STAY

Domaine des Hauts de Loire: part of the
sumptuous Relais et Châteaux group, this castle
and its former hunting lodge face Chaumont
across the Loire. Rooms in both look out onto
the impressive grounds, and there's a beautiful
outdoor pool. www.domainehautsloire.com

Chartres | Châteaudun | Chambord | Chaumont-sur-Loire | Amboise | Chenonceaux | Bourges

Chelsea

RHS Chelsea Flower Show

This world-famous flower show is a traditional highlight of the social season and a particular favourite of the Royal Family.

Organised by the Royal Horticultural Society (RHS) and dating back to the mid-19th century, the Chelsea Flower Show takes over the grounds of The Royal Hospital for five days each May, displaying a huge array of plants, plus a multitude of gardening accessories and tools.

New plant launches, more than 20 show gardens predicting coming trends, and flower-arranging demonstrations are among the offerings, and awards are given for categories such as Best Chic Garden and Best City Garden. The popularity of this show means that advance booking is essential.

OTHER FLOWER SHOWS
Harrogate Spring Flower Show
This non-RHS show takes place in April (followed by an Autumn Show in September) at the Great Yorkshire Showground and lasts four days. www.flowershow.org.uk

Stay and eat at nearby Rudding Park, a four-star hotel and golf resort with an award-winning restaurant. www.ruddingpark.com

Hampton Court Palace
A classic RHS flower show held in July. www.rhs.org.uk/hamptoncourt

Tatton Park, Cheshire
Held in July, with inspirational show gardens, competitions and 'growing and showing' stands. www.rhs.org.uk/tatton

STAY
Draycott Hotel. This luxury boutique hotel is a peaceful haven between Chelsea and Knightsbridge, with just 35 elegant rooms and suites, many with working fireplaces and some with garden views. www.draycotthotel.com

EAT
Bibendum. A long-standing favourite in a landmark Art Deco building first occupied by the Michelin Tyre Company Ltd, Bibendum is renowned for its French-accented seafood dishes, which you can also enjoy in its ground-floor Oyster Bar. www.bibendum.co.uk

Cannes Film Festival

Red carpets, palm trees, stars of the silver screen and their attendant paparazzi – the world's most famous film festival brings added glitter to one of the most chic resort towns in the South of France.

Now going strong for more than 60 years, Cannes is one of the world's longest-running film festivals, as well as one of the most influential. Usually held in May, it is focused around the 'Official Selection', which includes 20 films competing for the coveted Palme d'Or, but thousands of films are screened over the 12 days, some with a small number of tickets available to the public. Otherwise, there's plenty of star-gazing to be enjoyed, as well as the Cinéma de la Plage, with performances of film music and showings of Cannes classics and non-competition films on Macé beach.

STAY
It's essential to book rooms well in advance of the festival. Favourite among the stars is the legendary Majestic Barrière, with its own beach and sunbathing pier.
www.lucienbarriere.com

"Cinema is the most beautiful fraud in the world."

Jean-Luc Godard

Explore:
the coast

GRASSE

o It takes up to an hour to drive north from Cannes to Grasse, famous for its scents since the 17th century, and offering not only perfume shops but a museum and tours of the perfume factories Fragonard, Galimard and Molinard. www.fragonard.com; www.galimard.com; www.molinard.com

MOUGINS

o Just 15 minutes from Grasse, set amidst pine, olive and cypress trees, with gorgeous views down over the Bay of Cannes. Picasso spent the last 15 years of his life here, but it's best known for its gastronomy – it's home to more than 50 gourmet restaurants, including Le Moulin de Mougins and Le Restaurant Candille. www.moulin-mougins.com; www.lemascandille.com

ANTIBES

o Another 15 minues away, visitors flock to this pretty coastal town to visit the Musée Picasso in Château Grimaldi, in which the artist once stayed. From here it's 12 km (7.5 miles) back west along the coast to Cannes. www.antibes-juanlespins.com

Hay Literary Festival

The world's biggest literature festival draws writers, critics, film-makers, musicians, comedians, historians, scientists, environmentalists and politicians to an otherwise sleepy little town famed for its second-hand bookshops.

Famously described by visitor Bill Clinton as 'the Woodstock of the mind', this literature and arts festival, dating back to 1987, takes over the Welsh town of Hay-on-Wye, picturesquely set in the Brecon Beacons National Park, for ten days in May and June. As well as book-related events featuring internationally acclaimed authors such as John Updike and Margaret Atwood, it includes debates, art exhibitions, live music, film previews and a children's programme.

Hay, which has a population of just 1,500, evolved into the world's first 'book town' in the 1970s and now boasts around 40 second-hand and antiquarian bookshops attracting half a million visitors a year.

STAY

In a stunning location not far from Hay, Gliffaes Country House Hotel is renowned for its fishing. It offers 23 traditionally styled rooms overlooking either the beautiful Usk Valley or its own impressive gardens. Its restaurant adheres to the global 'Slow Food Movement', which espouses regional food and local producers. www.gliffaeshotel.com

HAY FESTIVAL GOERS
— GO THE EXTRA MILE! VISIT —
JESS & HEL'S
GARDEN
CAFE!

open daily from
10am onwards.

TEAS, COFFEES, &
FUNKY HOMEMADE CAKES
Some car
parking
available. Live Music Daily

BOOTH BOOKS

HAY

HAY CASTLE

→

FRAGMENTS OF MANUSCRIPTS

JOHN UZZELL EDWARDS
NEW PAINTINGS
AT THE DRILL HALL
HAY FESTIVAL SHOW

33

SPRING

34

BATH LITERATURE FESTIVAL

More than 100 events, from debates and
workshops to film screenings, bring novelists,
poets, journalists, scriptwriters, biographers,
actors, comedians and politicians from
Britain and abroad flocking to the UNESCO
World Heritage Site of Bath over nine days
in February and March. Bath's literary
credentials date back to the 18th century
and its association with novelist Jane Austen.
www.bathlitfest.org.uk

STAY: the five-star Macdonald Bath Spa offers
contemporary styling in a secluded Georgian
manor, plus a new spa, an indoor pool and
a croquet lawn.
www.macdonaldhotels.co.uk/bathspa

OXFORD LITERARY FESTIVAL

Around 250 writers flock to the famous
university city to discuss affairs literary,
political, environmental and culinary – to
name just a few – for this six-day festival
in late March or early April, hosted by the
atmospheric Christ Church College with its
Tudor hall and cloisters. Visitors can book
to join lunches and dinner parties with
prominent authors and, in 2008, a creative
writing course was added to the programme.
www.sundaytimes-oxfordliteraryfestival.co.uk

UK Literary Festivals

Book lovers in the UK can choose from a vast array of festivals throughout the year, many of them world-class.

STAY: Le Manoir aux Quat'Saisons. This country hotel and restaurant owned by the world-renowned chef Raymond Blanc has astonishing gardens and beautiful rooms and suites, all individually designed. Cookery courses are available. www.manoir.com

PORT ELIOT LIT FEST

This book event is held in the 18th-century landscaped park and walled garden of a Cornish stately home each July. It has some of the ambience of a music festival – as well as writing and poetry, there is a strong emphasis on live music performances and visitors can pitch tents for free or stay in Podpads (little plywood huts) or teepees. www.porteliotlitfest.com

STAY: a few miles north of Port Eliot, Devon's Hotel Endsleigh offers sumptuous accommodation in a former shooting and fishing lodge on the fringes of Dartmoor National Park. www.hotelendsleigh.com

LEDBURY POETRY FESTIVAL

Spread over ten days in July, Britain's biggest poetry festival takes over a medieval market town in the Malvern Hills boasting many links with poets over the centuries. On the agenda are readings, performances and talks by contemporary poets and actors, workshops, exhibitions, live music and walks, and there's an international poetry competition judged by each year's poet-in-residence. www.poetry-festival.com

STAY: Colwall Park. This country house hotel in a tranquil setting at the foot of the Malvern Hills has pretty gardens and direct access to good walking, plus an award-winning restaurant. www.colwall.co.uk

CHELTENHAM FESTIVAL OF LITERATURE

This large festival in the Gloucestershire Regency town offers events involving more than 400 writers and other speakers over ten days in October, including specially commissioned works by major writers as part of the MultiStory project. New theatre and visual arts displays are also on the programme, plus street performances around the town. Comedy and children's events are particularly strong. www.cheltenhamfestivals.com

STAY: Thirty Two is a Regency townhouse boutique hotel, located on Cheltenham's Imperial Square. The owners specialise in interior design and rooms offer exquisite furnishings. www.thirtytwoltd.com

"Choose an author as you choose a friend."

Sir Christopher Wren

Glyndebourne
Festival Opera

The famous East Sussex opera festival presents the perfect opportunity to indulge in champagne picnics on summer lawns.

Dating back more than 70 years, this world-class festival attracts scores of opera-lovers from London and further afield, especially for its Mozart, Handel and Janáček, staged in the acoustically brilliant multi-million pound modern auditorium that opened in the 1990s.

Landowner John Christie, who inherited the historic country house (probably 16th-century), and his opera-singer wife Audrey Mildmay originally set up the festival as a showcase for small-scale productions of Mozart operas.

The London Philharmonic is the main resident orchestra for the duration of the festival. Operas – about six in total, staggered throughout the summer months from May to August – commence in the afternoon and are punctuated by a lengthy 90-minute interval during which dinner can be taken on the large lawns, in the form of a picnic, or in one of the restaurants within the grounds.

Picnics, which can be pre-ordered along with porter service and furniture if required, feature the likes of champagne, lobster salad and Glyndebourne summer pudding.

STAY
Newick Park. This is a modern take on a country house hotel, with an intimate feel and fine dining, set in its own peaceful park with views over the South Downs. Glyndebourne is just 15 minutes away. www.newickpark.co.uk

EAT
The Jolly Sportsman. This excellent gastropub-cum-restaurant boasts contemporary art on its walls, a candlelit terrace with Moroccan tables, jasmine and clematis, and a pretty rear garden for light lunches, with South Down views. Food is seasonally inspired and locally sourced. www.thejollysportsman.com

"An opera begins long before the curtain goes up and ends long after it has come down."

Maria Callas

Prague
Spring International Music Festival

Make Prague's famous music festival the finale of a fascinating eastern European drive, linking fairytale castles, glorious palaces and quaint medieval towns.

Some of the world's foremost musicians, symphony orchestras and chamber music ensembles head to Prague for this musical showcase that began more than 60 years ago. Lasting about three weeks, the festival always opens with Smetana's 'My Country' cycle of symphonic poems on 12 May, the anniversary of the Czech composer's death, and ends with Beethoven's Symphony No 9.

In between you can also catch works that commemorate various anniversaries and premières of contemporary compositions.

Events are held in a variety of atmospheric and impressive venues, including the Neo-Renaissance Rudolfinum – a lavish concert hall by the Vltava river – a cinema, and various churches and convents, gving you a golden opportunity to explore the city.

Drive:
the Castle Road

The picturesque Burgenstrasse between Germany and Prague takes in 1,000 km of historical sites and fabulous scenery.

STAY
The Mandarin Oriental is a super-luxurious
option in a restored monastery just below
Prague castle, with a baroque Grand
Ballroom and a holistic spa within
a former Renaissance chapel.
www.mandarinoriental.com/prague

MANNHEIM

○ The starting point of the drive is home
to the Kurfürstliches Schloss or Electoral
Palace, Europe's biggest Baroque palace
complex, begun in 1720. Don't miss the
Great Hall with its impressive stucco
and ceiling frescoes.

HEIDELBERG

○ Heidelberg, with its lovely Old Town,
boasts a complex of palace and garden
architecture built over several centuries
by the Palatine Electors who were
based here. Events hosted at Schloss
Heidelberg and within its courtyard
include a castle festival each summer.

NECKARSTEINACH

○ Of the four castles here, the most
interesting is Burg Schadeck,
nicknamed the Swallow's Nest for the
way it perches high on the mountain.
The walkway along the top of the
curtain wall has panoramic views.

ROTHENBURG

○ This former free imperial city has a
picturesque walled medieval old town
with stunning valley views and a variety
of fascinating museums, including
one devoted to crime and punishment.
Allow two to three hours to walk around
the historic city walls.

BAYREUTH

○ As well as two palaces and the former
courtly retreat of the Eremitage,
Bayreuth is famous for its Festival
Theatre, hosting mainly Wagner operas.
Among the wonderfully atmospheric
places to stop and eat along the Castle
Road are the town's Schlossgaststätte
& Hotel Eremitage.
www.eremitage-bayreuth.de

KARLOVY VARY

○ The biggest Czech spa town (known
to Germans as Carlsbad), popular
for its mineral waters for 600 years,
is also famed for its china and glass.

Mannheim | Heidelberg | Neckarsteinach | Rothenburg | Bayreuth | Karlovy Vary | Prague

40

Bath
International Music Festival

One of Britain's most prestigious music festivals is also one of its most eclectic, presenting a mix of classical, contemporary, jazz, world, electronica and folk music.

THE FESTIVAL

For over sixty years, the Bath International Music Festival has looked to both the past and the future with its broad scope of musical styles. Performances are hosted in a wide variety of beautiful historic venues within Somerset's historic city, a UNESCO World Heritage Site that was founded as Aquae Sulis, location of a Roman baths and temple, and later became a Georgian spa resort (its famous crescents date from this time). These venues include Bath Abbey, a former Benedictine monastery where Edgar was crowned King in the 10th century, the Pump Rooms (a neo-classical salon within the redeveloped baths) and the Assembly Rooms, National Trust-owned public spaces used for fashionable functions in the 18th century. Some events are held outdoors, not least the free opening night celebration with fireworks, and the free outdoor show in the city centre on the final night.

STAY

The Bath Priory. This hotel, Michelin-starred restaurant and spa merits at least a weekend's stay, with its indoor and outdoor pools, fine paintings and antiques, and 27 individually designed rooms each named after a flower. www.thebathpriory.co.uk

Thermae Bath Spa boasts the only natural thermal waters in Britain. Visit this unique day spa and enjoy a treatment followed by unparalleled views of the city from the spa's rooftop pool. www.thermaebathspa.com

The long, balmy days of summer offer a dazzling array of possibilities. Festivals proliferate all over Europe, celebrating an eclectic range of activities, from opera, theatre and jazz to bull-running, tomato-throwing and balloon-flying. Summer sports offer spectators everything from the slow-burning intensity of a cricket Test match to the theatrical climax of the Wimbledon final. Traditional events, including the Henley Royal Regatta and Royal Ascot, hark back to the elegance of another era, while festivals such as Glastonbury and Edinburgh are both exciting and contemporary.

Summer

"Summer afternoon
– summer afternoon;
to me those have
always been the
two most beautiful
words in the English
language."

Henry James

Summer
Opera

46

Opera

Opera lovers can immerse themselves in top-notch musical events and festivals throughout the summer.

GARSINGTON OPERA

This month-long event in June/July is popular above all for its location, in the Italian-style gardens of Garsington Manor in Oxford, built in the 17th century but made famous by its links with the Bloomsbury set. The stage occupies the terrace and loggia attached to the manor, with the auditorium sheltered by a canopy. As at Glyndebourne, there's a long interval for guests to picnic or dine in the restaurant; prior to the performance one can take tea or champagne on the lawns. Established in 1989 to explore the neglected works of Haydn, Rossini, Richard Strauss and other celebrated composers, Garsington will be relocating after the 2010 season but will continue to present its diverse programme in a new home. www.garsingtonopera.org
STAY: Hartwell House. This hotel, restaurant and spa occupies a restored stately home in parkland near Aylesbury, 20 minutes from Garsington. www.hartwell-house.com

BUXTON FESTIVAL

The 17-day-long Buxton Festival is one of Britain's biggests arts festivals. It draws around 35,000 people to the Peak District town each July to watch a number of rarely staged operas, from the baroque period to contemporary pieces, performed in English. Past coups have included the UK premières of obscure works by Mozart, Rossini and Handel. A Literary Series runs in tandem with the opera programme, featuring talks by prominent novelists, biographers, political authors and others, and evenings see film screenings and various cultural events. In August Buxton also hosts the International Gilbert & Sullivan Festival of light opera. www.buxtonoperahouse.org.uk
STAY: The Palace Hotel. This imposing hotel in the heart of Buxton retains some of its Victorian-era charm, but now also boasts a modern indoor pool and treatment rooms. www.barcelo-hotels.co.uk

GRANGE PARK OPERA

Hampshire's Grange Park, a ruined early 19th-century Greek revival house in magnificent countryside, is the dramatic setting for this smaller-scale festival inaugurated in the late 1990s. Around five different operas are staged each June and July, in a new and award-winning theatre constructed within the old Orangery in 2003. The long interval allows time for dinner at Grange House, amidst *trompe l'oeil* hangings and chandeliers. Alternatively, picnics can be taken in a marquee or an Indian pavilion; if weather permits, the terraces, with their sweeping views over the parkland, are ideal. www.grangeparkopera.co.uk
STAY: Lainston House Hotel. This elegant 17th-century house, complete with courtyard, archways and loggias, nestles amidst manicured lawns, extensive woodlands, tennis courts and its own kitchen garden, and boasts lovely countryside views. www.lainstonhouse.com

"Is the air ever normal at Garsington? No, I think even the sky is done up in pale yellow silk…"

Virginia Woolf

Cricket Test Matches

Redolent of long, langorous summer days and traditional picnic teas yet packed with edge-of-the-seat drama, Test cricket inspires devotion among spectators around the globe, not least in the country in which the sport took seed.

Dating back to at least the 13th century and England's national summer sport by the late 18th century, cricket finds its ultimate expression – and sternest competition – in Test matches. The latter began during the English cricket team's tour of Australia in 1877 and now involves ten nations. The Ashes, the biennial Test series between Australia and England, remains cricket's most famous incarnation in the UK.

Ninety-five grounds worldwide have played host to Test matches including, in Britain:

> "I tend to think that cricket is the greatest thing that God ever created on earth. . ."
>
> Harold Pinter

LORD'S

'The Home of Cricket', Lord's in north London was founded in 1787 and is owned by the influential Marylebone Cricket Club. If two touring teams are visiting the UK, there will usually be two Tests played at Lord's in the summer, including the first of the season. Lord's prides itself on being the guardian of the Laws of Cricket, and the world's oldest sporting museum is to be found here, as well as stunning architecture, both traditional (the Victorian Pavilion) and modern (the futuristic pod of the Media Centre), plus a well-known weather vane in the shape of Father Time. Good views over the famously sloping field are found in the upper tiers of the Grand and the Mound Stands, although these are debentures and hence not readily available to the public; next best are Grand Stand seats. www.lords.org

STAY: The Dorset Square Hotel. An apt choice on the square where Lord's was first situated, with traditional county house décor – original fabrics and antique furniture, including four-posters, in some of the 37 rooms and suites. www.dorsetsquare.co.uk

TRENT BRIDGE

Nottingham's county cricket ground is one of Test cricket's oldest venues (the ground was founded in 1841), and played host to England versus Australia in 1899, the first match of England's first five-match test series. W.G. Grace, who was then 50 years old, played in this match, the last of his illustrious Test career. Many cricket fans deem Trent Bridge one of the world's best grounds for spectators; features range from an 1889 pavilion to the modernistic Fox Road Stand with its roof resembling an aircraft wing. The ground had a new stand plus extra seating created for the 2008 Test match with New Zealand. It can now host 15,000 spectators, and is regularly sold out on big cricketing occasions. The Radcliffe Road Stand provides excellent views of the ground. The venue also has one of Britain's finest state-of-the-art scoreboards, proffering an array of statistics. www.trentbridge.co.uk

STAY: The Lace Market Hotel, Nottingham's only boutique hotel, is located in the city centre and has received many accolades. www.lacemarkethotel.co.uk

atches

THE OVAL

South London's international cricket ground was a market garden when it was leased to Surrey County Cricket Club in 1845. Described as 'the Grand Old Lady' for its role in modern sports (football and Rugby Union used to be played there as well), it is usually host to the last Test match of the British summer. It is home to Surrey County Cricket Club, which was established in 1845, and was the first British ground to host a Test match (in 1882). The largest of Britain's Test grounds, it is famous for its mid-19th-century gasometers. In 2005 a new four-tier grandstand (the OCS) increased the ground's capacity, and its Upper Balcony provides excellent views. At the time of writing, plans for further redevelopment are underway. The Oval has a 23,000 all-seater capacity. www.surreycricket.com/the-brit-oval
STAY: 51 Buckingham Gate. Just a few steps from the Palace and St James's Park, these 5-star suites and apartments, many overlooking an historic courtyard, boast an organic spa and a variety of on-site fine dining opportunities. www.51-buckinghamgate.com

HEADINGLEY

Home to Yorkshire County Cricket Club (plus Leeds' rugby league and rugby union teams at an adjoining ground sharing the main stand), Leeds' Headingley Carnegie Stadium first hosted Test cricket in 1899. In 1930 Headingley witnessed Donald Bradman's epoch-making innings of 334 in the Ashes Test. In 1981 England beat Australia by 18 runs here, providing what some claim to be Test cricket's most incredible reversal (odds were 500-1 against an England victory). Current seating capacity at the ground is 17,000; redevelopment plans were announced in 2006. The newly renovated ground will be renamed the Headingley Carnegie Stadium; its seating capacity will increase to 20,000 and ambitious plans include a £12 million new pavilion and Media Centre.
www.yorkshireccc.com
STAY: Quebecs. Voted one of the world's top 80 hotels by *Condé Nast Traveller*, chic Quebecs occupies a Grade II listed building and boasts Victorian furnishings, stained-glass windows, wood panelling and understated classic décor. www.theetoncollection.com

EDGBASTON

Situated in central Birmingham and home to Warwickshire County Cricket Club, Edgbaston Cricket Ground was inaugurated in 1886 and first hosted Test cricket in 1902. The Eric Hollies stand, completed in 2002, is popular among spectators; the stadium's most famous sight remains the Thwaite Memorial Scoreboard, built in 1950. Further development, including a new pavilion to increase capacity, is planned. Brian Lara's record-breaking innings of 501 not out against Durham took place at Edgbaston in 1994. England won one of its closest Ashes victories here in 2005, with Australia losing by just two runs. England went on to win the Ashes that summer. In 1997 Edgbaston hosted the first ever floodlit evening game in England. www.edgbaston.com
STAY: Hotel du Vin. This member of the outstanding and award-winning small chain, occupying a handsome Victorian building in the city's fashionable Jewellery Quarter, offers not only luxurious accommodation, great food and wine and a spa, but also residential wine courses. www.hotelduvin.com

Arts Festivals

Summer is enlivened by arts events in a range of settings, from urban Dublin to the wilds of Orkney, the shores of the Mediterranean and the banks of the River Thames.

ST MAGNUS FESTIVAL

Founded in 1977 by resident Orkney composer Sir Peter Maxwell Davies, this adventurous midsummer festival brings arts lovers to the 'mainland' of the Scottish archipelago – a UNESCO World Heritage Site – for a five-day feast of world-class music, theatre, dance, visual arts and literature. Artists and companies as distinguished as André Previn, Evelyn Glennie, the Royal Philharmonic and the London Sinfonietta have graced the programme over the years, but the organisers are also active in commissioning up-and-coming young composers. There's an equal stress on commissioning new work in the fields of drama, dance and the visual arts. But perhaps most impressive of all is the festival's emphasis on participation by the local community, both adults and children, particularly in its Festival Chorus featuring about 100 Orkney singers.

The Orkney archipelago, comprising roughly 70 islands, of which 19 are inhabited, has a rich musical tradition and thriving small-scale crafts industries. Its vast beaches and soaring cliffs guarantee a wealth of bird- and sea-life, and the land is studded with Neolithic remains.
www.stmagnusfestival.com
STAY: Balfour Castle on the island of Shapinsay, a 25-minute ferry ride from Orkney Mainland, has Victorian furniture, blazing log fires and turrets in some guest-rooms. Private boat tours of nearby uninhabited islands and caves are available. www.balfourcastle.co.uk

BLOOMSDAY (LÁ BHLOOM)

A secular holiday in Ireland, Bloomsday is held on 16 June, the anniversary of the day when James Joyce went on his first date with his future wife Nora Barnacle, and is named after Leopold Bloom, the main character in Joyce's most famous novel, *Ulysses*. Events in Dublin (there are other Bloomsday events in the States and in Hungary) begin a week ahead of Bloomsday itself. Celebrating both Joyce's life and the novel itself, the action of which takes place over one day in Dublin in 1904, they include readings and dramatisations, pub crawls, street parties and 'Bloomsday Breakfasts', with much activity centred around the James Joyce Centre in North

> "To see the summer sky is poetry, though never in a book it lie."
>
> Emily Dickinson

Great George's Street. Some participants
even dress in Edwardian costume.
www.jamesjoyce.ie
STAY: The Merrion, a gracious hotel in the
centre, has classically appointed rooms,
a spa and infinity pool, and two restaurants.
www.merrionhotel.com

HENLEY FESTIVAL OF MUSIC & ARTS

Twenty-five years old in 2007, the Henley
Festival – described as 'the summer's
greatest party' – is held over five atmospheric
July evenings on the banks of the Thames
about 65 km (40 miles) west of London, with
visitors able to enjoy outdoor performances
of music, dance and street theatre (some of
them on a floating stage), visual arts displays
and a firework finale accompanied by music.
Classical music and jazz are imaginatively
backed up by the likes of Bahamian carnival
bands and Korean ceremonial drumming.
As much a part of the experience are the
alfresco eating and drinking opportunities
in a variety of settings, whether it be the
Riverside Restaurant presided over by Albert
Roux, the Champagne Terrace or the Italian
Piazza. Luxury picnics can be pre-ordered.
www.henley-festival.co.uk
STAY: for Henley hotels, see p.91.

FESTIVAL D'AIX-EN-PROVENCE

Under idyllic Provençal skies, this scenic town, popular with some of the world's greatest artists, thrills audiences with its ever-evolving opera repertoire.

Aix's opera festival, held annually in late June and July and on a par with that of Glyndebourne (see pp.36–37), celebrated its 60th anniversary in 2008. Its focus has varied over the years according to the director; since 1998, under Stéphane Lissner, it has commissioned several new operas and featured world-class classical concerts too, most notably the Berlin Philharmonic playing Mahler's 5th Symphony, and Pierre Boulez both conducting and playing the piano.

Among the various venues are the outdoor Théâtre de l'Archevêché, the restored courtyard of the former archbishop's palace, and the more intimate Hôtel Maynier d'Oppède. In 2007 the opening of the Grand Théâtre de Provence made it possible for attendance to increase by more than a third, to more than 80,000 people. The Académie Européenne de Musique, a summer school associated with the festival, hosts masterclasses for young talent by renowned musicians.

When you feel like taking a break from the music, explore the famous Cours Mirabeau, an avenue lined with pavement cafés and bookshops. In the height of the summer plane trees provide welcome shade. www.festival-aix.com

Explore: *Montagne Ste-Victoire*

Just east of Aix, this 1,011-metre (3,317-ft) mountain is famous for its link with painter
Paul Cézanne, for whom it was a favourite motif. The road encircling it offers wonderful
views and departure points for walks, and is dotted with picturesque villages dwarfed
by the summit, the Pic des Mouches (Peak of the Flies).

AIX-EN-PROVENCE
○ Your starting and finishing point.

THE SOUTH-WESTERN SLOPES
○ In Le Tholonet, a village on the mountain's steep south-westerly
slopes, you will find a windmill and a réfuge (mountain hut) used
by Cézanne, as well as an 18th-century castle that he painted.
Footpaths lead up to a ruined Roman viaduct above Le Tholonet,
as well as the Barrage Zola, a dam built by the novelist's father.
This side of the mountain is also home to the Roques-Hautes
departmental park, with hiking trails, a geology reserve,
prehistoric remains and a marble quarry.

ST-ANTONIN-SUR-BAYON
○ This village to the east of Le Tholonet, reached by a snaking
mountainside road, is home to the Maison de Ste-Victoire.
There's an exhibition on the area's wildlife and geology and
a shop selling local produce, books and guides. The remains
of a Roman settlement lie on a nearby plateau, as well as
La Croix de Provence, a cross from which there's a panoramic
view over the mountain and surrounding plains.

VAUVENARGUES
○ Driving around the eastern slopes you'll find the scenic villages
of Puyloubier and Pourrières, surrounded by vineyards. At the foot
of the mountain's northern slopes, Vauvenargues is overlooked
by a 14th-century château that was bought by Picasso in 1958; it
is in its grounds (not open to visitors) that the artist was buried.

STAY
The characterful Château de la Pioline, five minutes from
Aix, offers spacious rooms, some with private gardens,
overlooking parkland and formal gardens. There's a pool
and a restaurant specialising in Provençal cuisine.
www.chateaudelapioline.fr

Route des
Grandes Alpes

One of the world's most dramatic drives takes you from sparkling Lake Geneva to the waters of the Mediterranean via more than a dozen lofty Alpine passes.

The revival of an historic route that was created in the early 1900s by the Touring Club de France, the Route des Grandes Alpes meanders over a 685-km (425-mile) course from Thonon on Lake Geneva to Menton on the French Riviera. On the way are 16 Alpine passes, of which six exceed 2,000 metres (6,560 ft). The route, which is open from June to mid-October each year, was first traversed by the *charabancs* and *omnibus* of the Paris Lyon Méditerranée company; today you might see anything from Vespas to sports cars along its course.

THONON-LES-BAINS TO ARÊCHES-BEAUFORT (135 KM)
- Main sights: the Pont du Diable ('Devil's Bridge'); Le Reposoir's Musée du Gypaète (bearded-vulture museum) and its charterhouse; the chalets of the Vallée du Doron.

ARÊCHES-BEAUFORT TO VALLOIRE (175 KM)
- Main sights: Beaufort's cheese co-op; the Roselend dam and reservoir; the Col d'Iseran, the highest pass in the Alps and one of its loveliest; the old streets of Ste-Foy Tarentaise; the view from Pointe Bellevarde (reached by cable-car from Val d'Isère).

VALLOIRE TO VARS (115 KM)
- Main sights: Valloire's 17th-century church; the view from the Col du Galibier; the Lautaret botanical garden; the Combeynot nature reserve; Monêtier's Musée d'art Sacré (museum of religious art); the fortified quarter of Briançon.

STAY

Accommodation along the route ranges from simple mountain refuges to four-star hotels. One of the most charming (indeed, it's an 'hôtel de charme') lies between the Col de l'Izouard and Colle de la Cayolle (that is, between 382 and 492 km): the eight-room Villa Morelia, a quirky Alpine château, has classically styled rooms, an outdoor pool and a spa. www.villa-morelia.com

VARS TO VALBERG (110 KM)

○ Main sights: the vast Fort de Tournoux; the 'Mexican' houses of the Vallée de l'Ubaye; the Gorges du Bachelard; the Pont de la Cascade ('Waterfall Bridge'); Estenc and the source of the Var.

VALBERG TO MENTON (130 KM)

○ Main sights: medieval Beuil; the picture-postcard Provençal village of Roubion; the 11th-century church of St-Dalmas-Valdeblore; the ramparts and gargoyles of Saint-Martin-Vésubie; Sospel's cathedral and bridge; the Mediterranean vista from Fort de Sainte-Agnès.

MENTON

○ This Riviera town, dubbed 'la perle de la France', is famed for its beautiful gardens, many of which are open to the public, and hosts an annual classical music festival (July–August) with performances taking place outdoors on the portico of the gorgeous baroque Basilica of St Michel. Of the three-star hotels here, the most inviting is the Hôtel Aiglon, with its light and airy décor, charming gardens and outdoor pool. www.festivalmusiquementon.com; www.menton.fr; www.hotelaiglon.net

55

"Auto racing, bull fighting and mountain climbing are the only real sports… all others are games."

Ernest Hemingway

Fast Cars

Crowds of thousands gather to witness the awesome sight of Formula One cars battling it out on some of the Europe's most challenging racetracks.

THE EUROPEAN GRANDS PRIX

The Formula One season, which runs from March to November around the globe, consists of a series of Grand Prix races, the results of which decide two annual World Championships: drivers and constructors. The first modern-day Formula One World Championship was held in 1950 and featured the Monaco, British, French, Italian and Belgian Grands Prix, amongst others. As well as annual Grands Prix in the following countries, there is a European Grand Prix at changing venues.

Britain

The British Grand Prix, considered one of the world's foremost motor racing events, is also the oldest continuously staged Grand Prix along with the Italian race, dating back to 1950. It is held at Silverstone Circuit in Northamptonshire which used to be one of the fastest Formula One tracks until it was modified in the early 1990s.

STAY & EAT: Fawsley Hall, an impressive Tudor manor surrounded by parkland designed by Capability Brown, has a suite in which Elizabeth I once stayed. Bedrooms have period features, and there's a restaurant, spa and tennis courts. www.fawsleyhall.com

Belgium

Belgium's Grand Prix is hosted by the Circuit de Spa Francorchamps racecourse, and was re-opened for the 2007 season after huge redevelopment works offering improved Paddock and garage facilities. The circuit, one of the most historic on the Grand Prix calendar, is popular among both spectators and drivers: it is challenging because of the Spa region's unpredictable weather, and because it is undulating and twisty yet very fast (the Eau Rouge corner and Blanchimont turn enjoy particular notoriety). The skill required and the good opportunities for overtaking have made it the scene of some memorable driving duels.

STAY & EAT: the Radisson SAS Palace Hotel is right next to Europe's oldest casino and boasts a private funicular to Les Thermes de Spa, with thermal baths, Turkish baths, saunas, treatment rooms and more. www.radissonsas.com

Germany

Since 2007, the German Grand Prix has alternated between two venues: the Nürburgring and the Hockenheimring.

The Hockenheimring is in Baden-Württemberg, in the Rhine Valley. The track, which dates back to 1965, famously cut through the surrounding forests; the echo of screaming F1 engines eerily lingering in the shadows long after teams had packed up and moved out. In 2004 the Hockenheimring was redeveloped to make it shorter and to redirect the racing action from the forest sections to a newly constructed spectator zone and grandstand, the latter of which was the result of heavy investment by Mercedes-Benz.

The original Nürburgring was an awesome 22-km (14-mile) monster that wound its way through the surrounding landscape and was the birthplace of the original Mercedes-Benz Silver Arrow racecar in 1934 (the silver metal bodywork gave rise to the name 'Silver Arrow' when the W25 had the white paint removed to lower its weight).

The track was dropped from the Grand Prix calendar in 1976 and an entirely new track was built for the 1984 season.

STAY & EAT: close to Hockenheim is the Steigenberger Hotel Mannheimer Hof, with luxurious modern rooms and a restaurant with a courtyard terrace. Nürburg is accessible to Cologne, and the luxury Hotel im Wasserturm in an old water tower, with modern rooms and a restaurant serving classic French fare. www.mannheim.steigenberger.com; www.hotel-im-wasserturm.de

France

The French Grand Prix is one of the oldest, dating back to 1906. It has taken place at the Circuit de Nevers Magny-Cours in rural Burgundy since 1991.

STAY & EAT: south-west of Nevers, Le Prieuré d'Orsan is a former priory with seven welcoming rooms and a renowned restaurant. www.prieuredorsan.com

Spain

The Spanish Grand Prix has been hosted by the Circuit de Catalunya in Montmeló not far north of Barcelona since 1991. Used as a testing ground by the Formula One teams, it offers a challenging combination of varied corners and straights with the added bonus of long daylight hours for maximum track time.

STAY & EAT: the Hotel Arts, a spectacular modern seafront high-rise with an outdoor pool, a spa and a Michelin-starred restaurant. www.hotelartsbarcelona.com

In 2008, Valencia, Spain's third largest city, hosted its first European Grand Prix. The 5.4-km (3.2-mile) circuit takes cars through the streets of the city, reaching top speeds of 200 mph. It skirts the harbour, recently reconstructed for the America's Cup, with a stunning panorama of the Mediterranean.

STAY AND EAT: Palau de la Mar, made up of two adjoining 19th-century mansions, has 66 elegant rooms, a patio and a restaurant serving excellent local cuisine. www.epoquehotels.com

Italy

Italy's Grand Prix is one of the world's oldest motor racing events, having begun at Brescia in 1921. In 1922 the mainly flat Autodromo Nazionale Monza was built in northern Italy and most races have been held there. One of the world's most famous tracks, it is distinguished by the fact that drivers are on full throttle for over 70 per cent of the lap thanks to the long straights, with cars able to reach speeds in excess of 372 km/h (231 mph).

STAY & EAT: Monza, just outside Milan, is home to the Hotel Principe di Savoia. A refined option dating from the 1920s, it has a pool and spa, and a famous restaurant serving Italian classics. www.hotelprincipedisavoia.com

Hungary

The Hungarian Grand Prix has been hosted at the Hungaroring in Mogyoród close to Budapest since its birth in 1986. The narrow twists and turns of the course, freqently dusty in hot weather, make for exciting races. Pit strategy is often key to success, as overtaking is challenging, despite modifications made to the course in recent years.

STAY & EAT: the Four Seasons Gresham Palace Budapest, is a famous landmark on the banks of the Danube, with views over the Buda hills. It is one of the finest examples of Art Nouveau in Central Europe, with beautifully restored ironwork and stained glass. It boasts a spa and infinity pool, and a modern Italian restaurant. www.fourseasons.com/budapest

Monaco

The Circuit de Monaco, which is built on the streets of Monte Carlo and La Condamine, is one of the most challenging Formula One tracks, with its many tight turns and changes in elevation. The Monaco Grand Prix is one of the most famous and popular; its wealthy setting also makes it one of the most glamorous. Dating back to 1929, it is part of the Triple Crown of Motorsport, together with the Indianapolis 500 and Le Mans 24 Hours.

STAY & EAT: the Hôtel Metropole. A classic palace-hotel, with landscaped gardens, a restaurant named after its famous chef Joël Robuchon, another restaurant beside the outdoor pool, and a spa. www.metropole.com

Turkey

The Turkish Grand Prix, held at the Istanbul Park Circuit, dates back only to 2005. The German-designed circuit – one of only three anti-clockwise circuits on the calendar – is considered to be one of the world's most exciting and demanding in that it follows the dips and falls in the land, and has a very difficult corner, Turn 8 – a multi-apex corner whereby the drivers are exposed to G-forces approximately five times the force of gravity.

STAY & EAT: situated on the European shores of the Bosphorus, The Four Seasons Bosphorus is an elegant 19th-century palace with extensive spa facilities, saunas, and men's and womens' *hammams* (Turkish baths). www.fourseasons.com/bosphorus

DTM

The Deutsche Tourenwagen-Meisterschaft (German Touring Car Championship) is Europe's most popular touring car race series, which began in 1984 with production based cars and peaked in 1996 with a worldwide series for high-tech touring cars. High costs meant that the series was discontinued, but after a three-year break, the DTM celebrated a successful comeback in the year 2000. The championship takes place between April and October, with most rounds of the 12-race series being held at German racetracks, with occasional rounds in other European locations, such as Brands Hatch, UK, and Le Mans, France. The Nürburgring and Hockenheim feature, but races also take place in Düsseldorf, Oschersleben and Norisring. The 2000 comeback featured Mercedes-Benz and Opel only; Audi joined the DTM in 2004. The road models used as patterns since then are Mercedes-Benz C-Class, the Opel Vectra GTS and the Audi A4. www.dtm.com

STAY & EAT:
NUREMBERG (NORISRING): Le Meridien Grand Hotel, situated at the gateway to the old city, offers opulent comfort.
www.starwoodhotels.com/lemeridien
DUSSELDORF: The Steigenberger Park Hotel is an imposing five-star option, set on a major boulevard. www.steigenberger.com
OSCHERSLEBEN: The Maritim Hotel in nearby Magdeburg is a stylish town centre hotel with pool and sauna. www.maritim.de

Polo

The fast-paced 'sport of kings' makes for a thrilling spectacle as well as some of the summer season's social highlights.

Britain's main polo season lasts from May to September, with indoor or arena polo played in winter. The sport – one of the world's oldest, dating back to at least 600 BC in Persia but adapted into its modern form in 19th-century India – has long had royal connections. Prince Philip was a key figure in its revival after the Second World War, Prince Charles has represented his country at polo, and his sons William and Harry are also keen players. Polo attracts an international crowd of horse-lovers from as far afield as Dubai and South America.

Played with giant mallets, polo can be dangerous. Outdoor games, which are faster than indoor ones, consist of up to eight seven-minute chukkas (from the Sanskrit *chakra*, meaning circle or wheel), between which players change mounts. There are four players on a team, each handicapped from -2 to 10; only about half a dozen players around the world hold the highest handicap of 10. The following top tournaments are all part of the World Polo Tour. Teams fight for a Subsidiary Trophy on the morning of the final day, and the real final takes place after lunch.

The Prince of Wales Trophy
This first high-goal (top-level professional) tournament of the season is held in late May or June at the atmospheric Royal County of Berkshire Club in Windsor, a polo complex with six grounds founded by music promoter Bryan Morrison in 1985.
www.rcbpoloclub.com

The Queen's Cup
Held in mid-June, the Queen's Cup is one of the fastest high-goal tournaments. It's held at Guards Polo Club in Windsor Great Park,

Europe's largest polo club, which has had the Duke of Edinburgh as its president since its inception in 1955. The Queen donated the trophy to the club in 1960 and still presents it to the winning team.
www.guardspoloclub.com

The Warwickshire Cup
The Cirencester Park Polo Club in Gloucestershire, Britain's oldest polo club (established in 1896), is the setting for this tournament in late June or early July. Hosted on an idyllic estate boasting

> "Playing polo is like trying
> to play golf during an earthquake."
>
> Sylvester Stallone

3,000 acres of parkland and woodland, its number one ground is the famous Ivy Lodge, claimed to be the best all-weather ground in England. www.cirencesterpolo.co.uk

The Gold Cup

The Gold Cup, which celebrated its 50th anniversary in 2006, is the highlight of the season at Cowdray Park, the home of British polo, set within an Area of Outstanding Natural Beauty on a vast estate in West Sussex. Considered to be one of the most glamorous social events of the sporting season, it attracts celebrities from various fields; VIP packages include a three-course lunch, grandstand seating with champagne and a traditional English tea. www.cowdraypolo.co.uk

Cartier International

Billed by its host venue, Guards Polo Club, as 'the biggest polo day in the world', the Cartier International attracts a crowd of around 25,000, including royalty, and Hollywood and rock stars, in late July. www.guardspoloclub.com

STAY

For the Runnymede Hotel & Spa near Windsor, see p.74.
Barnsley House near Cirencester has stylish modern rooms.
The Cowdray Estate has its own holiday cottages; guests can enjoy clay-pigeon shooting and fly-fishing. In nearby Midhurst, the Spread Eagle is an old coaching inn with a spa, pool and 'modern classic' food.
www.barnsleyhouse.com;
www.cowdray.co.uk; www.hshotels.co.uk

Brecon Jazz Festival

The lovely scenery of the Brecon Beacons National Park forms a fitting backdrop for one of the world's foremost jazz festivals.

Twenty-five years old in August 2008, the Brecon Jazz Festival attracts some of the best international talent in the field and an audience of up to 70,000 to an idyllic setting in a pretty market town in Powys, mid Wales. As well as three days of performances of all kinds of jazz and related music in the main venues – from New Orleans funk and rhythm and blues to big band and European contemporary – the convivial atmosphere is enhanced by free street music and a parallel Brecon Fringe Festival of concerts in local pubs and clubs.

Entry to the major concerts is by ticket only, and it's wise to book well in advance. For 'stroller music' (roughly 50 events by lesser-known acts) visitors can buy wristbands for one day or the whole festival. STAY: many people choose to camp at the festival. Alternatively, Peterstone Court is a country house hotel and organic spa with an outdoor pool. Some of the food comes directly from the family farm nearby. www.peterstone-court.com

www.breconjazz.co.uk

Drive: *the Brecon Beacons*

Explore the wild beauty of this remote region.

BRECON
o Your starting point, on the edge of the National Park, has a cathedral, an 18th-century inn, a riverbank promenade and boat hire on the picturesque Monmouthshire and Brecon Canal.

BRECON BEACONS MOUNTAIN CENTRE
o Ten km (6 miles) southwest of Brecon at Libanus, this is a charming spot with waterfalls, old viaducts, castles, caves and nature walks, as well as the park's main visitor centre.

LLANGORS LAKE
o Just to the east of Brecon lies this protected wildlife site and boating and fishing spot, with a bird hide, a viewing platform and an ancient crannog (an artificial island used as a settlement).

TRETOWER
o This little town is distinguished by its three-storey round keep, dating from the 13th century when it was part of a castle, and the well-preserved late medieval fortified Tretower Court.

HAY-ON-WYE
o The famous book town is the site of a literary festival in May–June (see pp.32–33), but most of its second-hand bookshops are open year round.

OTHER BRITISH JAZZ FESTIVALS
March: Gateshead International Jazz Festival www.thesagegateshead.org
April: Isle of Wight International Jazz Festival www.iowjazzfestival.co.uk
April/May: Cheltenham Jazz Festival www.cheltenhamfestivals.com
July: Birmingham International Jazz Festival www.birminghamjazzfestival.com
July: Swanage Jazz Festival www.swanagejazz.org.uk
July/August: Edinburgh Jazz & Blues Festival www.edinburgh-festivals.com/jazzblues
November: London Jazz Festival www.londonjazzfestival.org.uk

European Jazz Festivals

July is a prime month for jazz lovers, with no fewer than four major European festivals.

NICE JAZZ FEST

Nice's eight-day festival offers a wide-ranging mix of jazz, from gospel and blues to urban funk, and from African roots to experimental sounds. It is also one of the world's most atmospheric jazz festivals, thanks to its charming setting in a 2,000-year old Gallo-Roman amphitheatre, the Arènes de Cimiez, nestling amongst olive groves. The gardens are also home to a Matisse museum, and the artist is buried in the Cimiez cemetery.

The Fest, which was set up in 1948, draws around 45,000 visitors, who can wander freely among three stages hosting simultaneous performances, which change hourly throughout the evening. www.nicejazzfest.com
STAY: the Hôtel Negresco, overlooking the Bay of Angels, is a private palace and National Historic Monument with an outstanding collection of French art. It offers flamboyant décor, a restaurant, a brasserie and a private beach. www.hotel-negresco-nice.com

UMBRIA JAZZ FESTIVAL

Held since 1973 and one of Europe's leading jazz events, the Umbria Jazz Festival takes over the Renaissance hill city of Perugia for ten days. It has always attracted big names, including Miles Davis, Dizzy Gillespie, Herbie Hancock and Keith Jarrett, together with an audience of more than 200,000 from around the world. Many performances take place outdoors, including those at the main venue, the 4,500-seat Giardini del Frontone, and the city's streets and squares host free shows by marching bands and blues, rock and gospel groups. www.umbriajazz.com

STAY: the hilltop Hotel Brufani Palace has attracted such guests as the Queen Mother and the Prince of Monaco. Rooms mix traditional décor with a clean, modern feel, and there's an amazing indoor pool with a transparent floor through which Etruscan remains can be seen. www.brufanipalace.com

MONTREUX JAZZ FESTIVAL

Montreux's two-week-long jazz festival is one of the world's best known, bringing fans of the genre, and of world music in general, flocking to Switzerland. Set up in 1967, it has featured an eclectic range of artistes, from

65

"There are wonderful things in real jazz, the talent for improvisation, the liveliness, the being at one with the audience."

Henri Matisse

Ella Fitzgerald and Count Basie to New Order and David Bowie – the programming has extended beyond jazz, although that does remain its focus.

Montreux is on the 'Swiss Riviera' on the banks of Lake Geneva, within easy reach of Geneva airport. The main festival venue is the Convention Centre, which has two major stages (the Stravinsky Auditorium and the Miles Davis Hall), the smaller Montreux Jazz Café, and some open-air stages. There are also performances in the original venue, the Casino, plus small-scale shows on boats plying the lake. www.montreuxjazz.com

STAY: the Fairmont Le Montreux Palace, a splendid Belle Epoque building with Alp and lake views, elegant rooms, four restaurants, indoor and outdoor pools and a spa. www.fairmont.com/montreux

NORTH SEA JAZZ FESTIVAL
Formerly held in The Hague, this three-day festival at the Rotterdam Ahoy arena in the Netherlands was set up in 1976, with the aim of bringing a wide range of jazz to the public, from American to European avant-garde. Having been expanded to incorporate 15 stages and drawing more than 20,000 music

fans a day, it aims to present something for everyone with its mix of New Orleans jazz, swing, bebop, fusion, blues, funk, soul and drum and bass. Jazz legends Sarah Vaughan and Stan Getz have appeared here.

The festival tends to sell out early; Early Bird tickets are available to regular visitors. www.northseajazz.com
STAY: there's a dedicated joint hotel and ticket booking service for the festival. The modern Westin Rotterdam is the city's only five-star hotel; spa treatments are available in-room. www.northseajazzhotels.com; www.westin.nl

Summer Surf

The wide open spaces of France's south-western Atlantic coast are famous for their
giant rollers; combine exhilarating surfing with fresh oysters and regional cuisine.

The Atlantic coast between Bordeaux and the border with Spain,
consisting of the Côte d'Argent and then the Côte Basque, is
dotted with countless small resorts to which surfers flock in search
of the best rollers. Surfing was first seen in France in the late 1950s,
when actors Dick Zanuck and Peter Viertel, husband of Deborah Kerr,
practised the sport while in Biarritz filming *The Sun Also Rises*.

Locals began to make their own boards, and surfing has since
become a local obsession, with board hire and surf schools found
in most coastal towns. In addition to the resorts already mentioned,
Soulac, Carcans-Océan, Biscarrosse, Moliets and Mimizan are popular
with both experts and beginners. There are many surfing competitions
during the summer months, especially at Biarritz, France's surf capital.

Drive: *the surf road*

Explore the dramatic coast of Aquitaine and enjoy some of Europe's best surf spots.

BORDEAUX
- Your starting or finishing point.

THE GIRONDE
- The Gironde region north of Bordeaux is where the Oxbow surfing brand was born in the 1980s. It's worth making a detour to the little resort of Montalivet if you're in the region in April, when the Monta Kokoloko surf club hosts the Coupe de Gironde 1. The Coupe de Gironde 2 is hosted at Le Porge-Océan, south towards Arcachon, in May – the same month as the Championnat de Gironde takes place at nearby Hourtin Plage. In August, Lacanau-Océan is the setting for the Sooruz Lacanau Pro and the Oakley Lacanau Junior Pro competitions.

ARCACHON
- Stop off at this seaside town southwest of Bordeaux to see Europe's biggest sand dune and to taste oysters from some of the 350 farmers who work on the Bassin d'Arcachon, providing almost two-thirds of the oysters consumed in France.

MESSANGES PLAGE
- In May this small resort hosts the Championnat des Landes competition at its Waiteuteu Messanges surf club.

CAPBRETON AND HOSSEGOR
- These are two of the best surfing beaches on the Côte d'Argent, located down towards Bayonne, each with a boardwalk and seafront cafés, restaurants and surf shops. In August/September, Hossegor – which has been home to the Fédération Française de Surf, founded in Biarritz, since 1984 – hosts the Rip Curl Pro, the Rip Curl Mademoiselle and Pro Junior Rip Curl Series competitions.

BIARRITZ
- This former fishing village has been dubbed the 'California of Europe'. Surfing schools and shops abound here. Among the many surf competitions hosted by Biarritz are the Quiksilver Pro surfing tournament for men and the Roxy Pro World Longboard tournament for women (September/October). There's also Les Têtards ('Headstrong') in August, a competition for rising stars aged 5–14. September sees the first leg of the Ocean Thunder Pro Surf Rowing competition on the Grande Plage. The French competition Bodysurf Challenge/Coupe de France takes place over several months, ending in October, while November sees the Championnats de France de Bodysurf.

STAY & EAT

The beachfront Hôtel du Palais at Biarritz was built by Napoleon III in 1854 as a private villa for his wife Eugenie. It has four restaurants, an indoor pool and spa and an outdoor heated pool.
www.hotel-du-palais.com

Aldeburgh Festival

68

Now going strong for more than 60 years, this festival on the Suffolk coast focuses on classical music but has expanded beyond its original remit to include literature, poetry, drama, lectures and art exhibitions.

Aldeburgh's distinctive arts festival was set up in 1948 by composer Benjamin Britten, singer Peter Pears and librettist Eric Crozier as a home for their opera company, but has since branched out into literature, theatre and the visual arts. It has always been active in seeking to present new pieces or interpretations and neglected works; several works by Britten have premièred here.

Held over 17 days in June, the festival takes place in various atmospheric venues in and around the coastal town of Aldeburgh but is centred on the concert hall just inland at Snape Maltings. The latter, which opened in 1967 and comprises a converted Victorian barley malthouse, is at the heart of a complex that also includes craft shops and boutiques, galleries, restaurants and cafés picturesquely situated alongside the Alde Estuary, part of an Area of Outstanding Natural Beauty with splendid wildlife.

69

STAY & EAT

The Swan in Southwold, north of Aldeburgh, is the classic choice in the area, with elegant rooms individually styled according to their view over the town. The restaurant focuses on seasonal ingredients, often organic, from local growers, farmers and fishermen, and there's a drawing room for afternoon teas. Its sister hotel a few steps away, The Crown, is famous for its food. www.adnams.co.uk/hotels

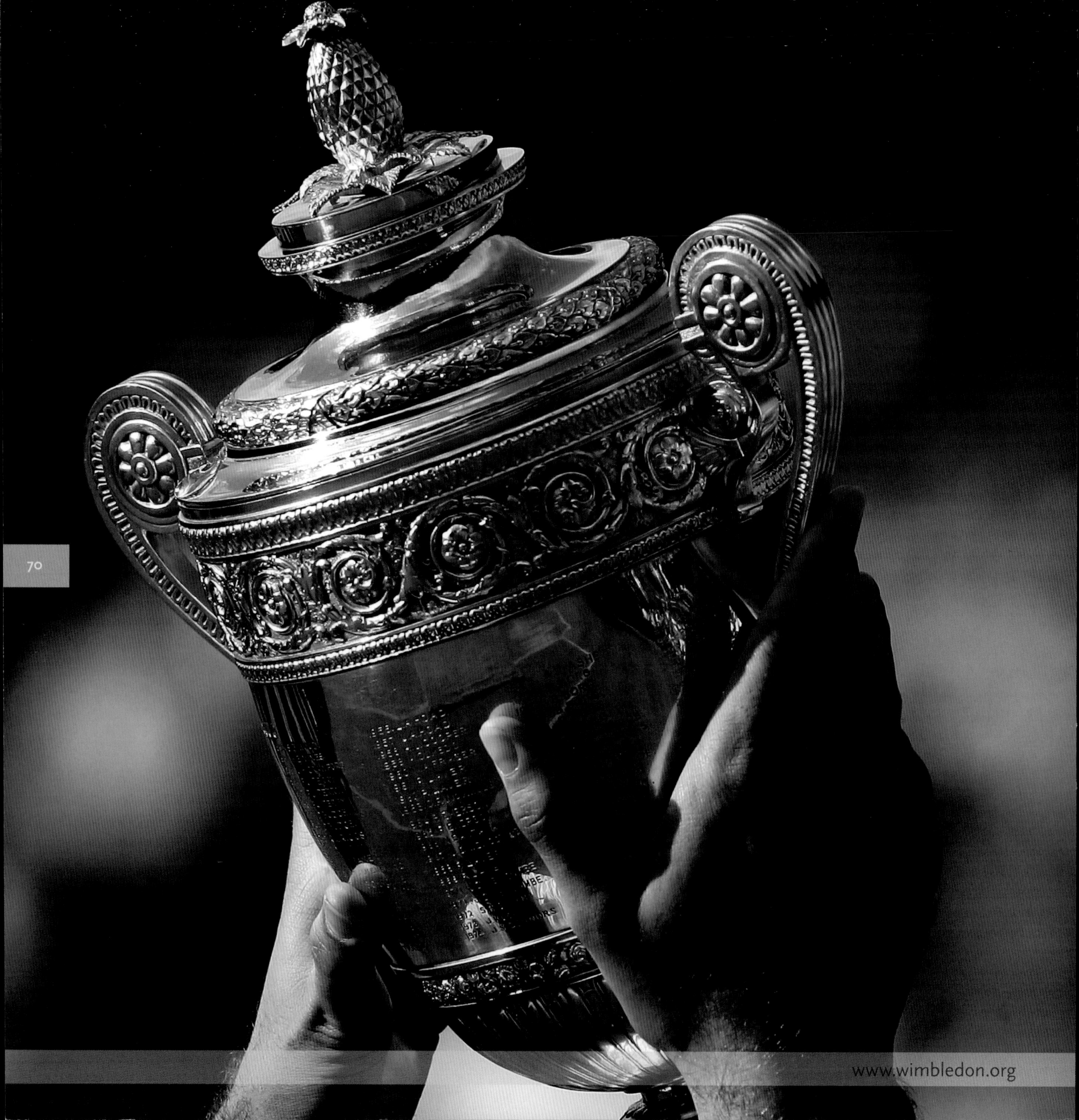

Wimbledon

This erstwhile garden-party tournament, which began in 1877, has grown to become one of the world's favourite sporting events.

The world's oldest major tennis championship, fought out for two weeks between late June and early July at south London's All England Lawn Tennis and Croquet Club, is the third Grand Slam tournament of the year and the only one still played on grass. The most important matches are played on the main Centre Court: improved for 2008 and, at the time of writing, due to have a new retractable roof for 2009. It hosts the semi-finals and finals of the main events (gentlemen's singles, ladies' singles, gentlemen's doubles, ladies' doubles and mixed doubles), plus many earlier round matches featuring top-seeded players.

Next down are No. 1 Court and No. 2 Court. Most tickets for these courts are sold in advance via a public ballot, entry for which closes in December. However, Wimbledon is the only major Grand Slam where fans can queue for tickets for the same day's matches on Centre Court, No. 1 Court and No. 2 Court (overnight queuing is generally required to guarantee a ticket).

The venue has a choice of restaurants and cafés, several of them selling the traditional Wimbledon snack of strawberries and cream, plus champagne and Pimm's.

There are six designated car parks, plus a park and ride shuttle-bus service from the A3.

"I've had a love affair with Wimbledon ever since I can remember. It stays with you."

Fred Perry

STAY
Petersham Hotel, situated on the side of Richmond Hill and affording views over the Thames and surrounding meadows, is a quiet retreat with a country house ambience and an award-winning restaurant. River-view rooms have balconies. www.petershamhotel.co.uk

EAT
Petersham Nurseries Restaurant and Tea House serves modern British food in an unusual English country garden setting near Richmond, from a kitchen presided over by *Vogue* food writer Skye Gyngell. www.petershamnurseries.com

Royal Ascot

Ascot stages 26 days of racing throughout the year, but the four-day Royal Meeting, held annually in June, is the most famous – a key date in the social calendar which combines venerable tradition with fashionable panache.

The first race meeting ever held at Ascot took place on 11 August 1711 and was instigated by Queen Anne, but it was with the accession of George II that the race became the second most popular in England.

Originally established to ensure privacy for members of the royal family, the Royal Enclosure dates back to the 1790s, when a separate Royal Stand was erected. The exclusive Royal Box, commissioned by George IV in 1822, was only accessible to guests brandishing a royal invitation.

Each day during the four-day Royal Meeting the Queen and her party drive in open-topped carriages across Windsor Park, entering the racecourse by the Golden Gates.

The prestigious Gold Cup event is held on Ladies' Day (Thursday), when women entering the Royal Enclosure must wear a hat that covers the 'crown of their head'.

DRESS CODES

THE ROYAL ENCLOSURE: to gain entry, race-goers must be recommended by someone who is already on the list. Convicted criminals and undischarged bankrupts are barred from the Royal Enclosure. Divorcées have been allowed in since 1955.

MEN: morning suit, national dress or uniform. Top hats and no brown shoes.

LADIES: hats and formal daywear – dresses and skirts that are no more than two inches above the knee. Trousers may only be worn as part of a suit. Bare legs are frowned upon. Stilettos are not recommended, as they make walking on grass difficult.

GRANDSTAND ENCLOSURE: visitors dress smartly for this occasion. Many ladies wear hats, although this is not obligatory. Gentlemen are required to wear a suit or jacket, in both cases with a tie.

Brooklands Motoring Festival: The Double Twelve

This new event thrills car enthusiasts, combining a world-class concours d'elégance with action-packed driving tests that hark back to the heyday of pre-war motoring.

Organised by Brooklands Museum and its neighbour, Mercedes-Benz World, near the Surrey town of Weybridge, the Brooklands Motoring Festival: The Double Twelve was inaugurated in 2007. Its name hails from 1930s Double Twelve meetings, when cars raced for 12 hours on consecutive days because 24-hour racing was not allowed.

Over a single weekend in late June, veteran, vintage and classic cars are judged for style, while their drivers are challenged on manoeuvres that were used in the 1939 Junior Car Club Rally. Other displays and special events might include Formula One demonstrations, helicopter displays and vintage bicycle races, including penny farthing racing, and there are all manner of stalls and street entertainment. Visitors can also see the motoring and aircraft collections within the Brooklands Museum, including Concorde.

Parade laps take place on the Mercedes-Benz World handling tracks next door, where festival-goers can take a passenger ride in a fabulous Mercedes-Benz AMG. The venue is open year-round for driving experiences on the various handling circuits, and has a 'discover' zone where visitors can learn about the history of the brand.

STAY
In Egham, the Runnymede Hotel & Spa offers comfortable rooms and apartments, with lawns overlooking the river.
www.runnymedehotel.com

"Motion is tranquility."

Sir Stirling Moss

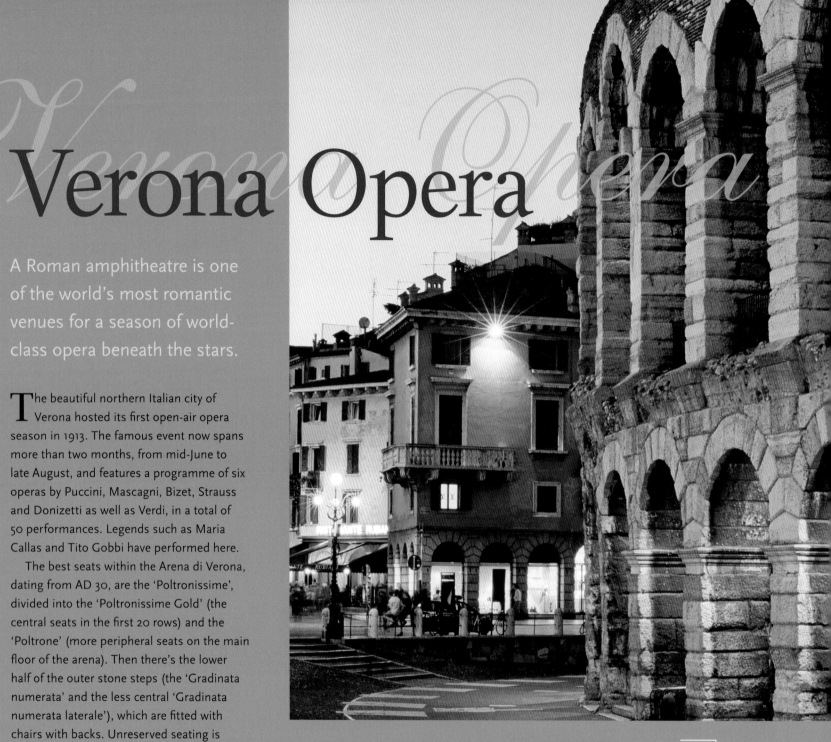

Verona Opera

A Roman amphitheatre is one of the world's most romantic venues for a season of world-class opera beneath the stars.

The beautiful northern Italian city of Verona hosted its first open-air opera season in 1913. The famous event now spans more than two months, from mid-June to late August, and features a programme of six operas by Puccini, Mascagni, Bizet, Strauss and Donizetti as well as Verdi, in a total of 50 performances. Legends such as Maria Callas and Tito Gobbi have performed here.

The best seats within the Arena di Verona, dating from AD 30, are the 'Poltronissime', divided into the 'Poltronissime Gold' (the central seats in the first 20 rows) and the 'Poltrone' (more peripheral seats on the main floor of the arena). Then there's the lower half of the outer stone steps (the 'Gradinata numerata' and the less central 'Gradinata numerata laterale'), which are fitted with chairs with backs. Unreserved seating is available on the higher stone steps (for which cushions can be hired), but get there early to bag a good spot.

Verona is a UNESCO World Heritage Site with various Roman remains and many notable medieval and Renaissance structures.

STAY & EAT

The elegant and central Due Torri Hotel Baglioni becomes home to many of the Verona Opera's stars each season, as well as having once welcomed Mozart. Its Art Nouveau restaurant, Brunello, is one of the best places to taste dishes from the surrounding Veneto region, as well as wider Italian and international cuisine. www.baglionihotels.com; www.brunellorestaurant.com

Drive: *around Lake Garda*

Although it's the largest lake in Italy, Garda can be comfortably toured in a day: its shoreline extends about 160 km (100 miles). Situated 28 km (17 miles) west of Verona, it has very varied scenery – rolling plains towards the south, vineyards around the central section, and Alpine peaks at the northernmost reaches.

SIRMIONE

- On a peninsula covered with olive and cypress groves at the southern end of the lake, Sirmione retains its Roman ruins and thermal springs, as well as a turreted castle.

DESENZANO

- At the south-western edge of the lake, this picturesque town is famous for its fine 4th-century Roman villa with striking mosaics. Just north of here are alluring beaches at Moniga and San Felice di Benaco.

GARDONE RIVIERA

- The highlight of this town is the one-time residence of poet and national hero Gabriele d'Annunzio, with its fantastical grounds and interiors, but there's also a botanical garden with modern art installations amidst natural wonders.

GARGNANO

- This beautiful village idolised by D.H. Lawrence is best known as the home of the luxurious Villa Feltrinelli hotel but is worth stopping at for its Michelin-starred restaurant La Tortuga.

RIVA DEL GARDA

- The lake's northernmost town has a cobbled historical centre with medieval towers, a 14th-century castle and Renaissance churches. It's a popular windsurfing spot.

MALCESINE

- On the eastern shore, take a cable-car from this delightful little port to the summit of Monte Baldo, which boasts some wonderful lake views.

BARDOLINO

- This pretty town, with its brightly coloured waterfront buildings, is a good spot to pick up some red wine from the surrounding vineyards before heading back to Verona. You can also explore numerous pretty lakeside villages by making use of the excellent local ferry and hydrofoil services.

Sirmione | Desenzano | Gardone Riviera | Gargnano | Riva del Garda | Malcesine | Bardolino

European Opera

At the height of summer, continental Europe offers up some captivating waterside venues for both popular and lesser-known operas.

> "No good opera plot can be sensible… people do not sing when they are feeling sensible."
>
> W.H. Auden

BREGENZ FESTSPIELE

On the Austrian shore of Lake Constance, Bregenz's month-long music and drama festival from late July to late August boasts the world's biggest floating stage, which seats an audience of 7,000 for lavish large-scale operas, usually from the popular repertoire (recent performances include Puccini's *La Bohème* and Bernstein's *West Side Story*). Other venues are the Festspielhaus, for neglected opera and concerts; the Werkstattbühne ('Workshop Theatre'), for contemporary opera and drama; the Theater am Kornmarkt, for operetta; and Martinsplatz, the medieval square in the scenic upper town, for open-air plays. The Festspielhaus is used as an indoor venue if the weather is changeable.

Founded in 1946, the festival has grown and diversified to comprise roughly 80 performances that draw more than 300,000 visitors to the historic town at the foot of Pfänder Mountain. www.bregenzerfestspiele.com

STAY & EAT: the 'gourmet-hotel' Deuring Schlössle has individually designed rooms and suites mixing antiques with modern designer furniture, one in a turret, and a beautiful restaurant. www.deuring-schloessle.at

LES AZURIALES OPERA

Cap Ferrat on the Côte d'Azur is the setting over two weeks each August for this intensely atmospheric opera festival, founded in 1997. It is a relatively intimate experience, with each of the ten or so evening performances – held in the round in the colonnaded and covered courtyard of the Belle Epoque Villa Ephrussi de Rothschild – open to only 200 guests. Even guests in the back row are closer to the performers than the conductor is in an opera house. Operas are sung in their original language, with English and French surtitles, and most performances are accompanied by just a piano rather than an orchestra. There is usually at least one Mozart opera on the programme.

After some performances, the artists join the audience for an alfresco late dinner in the gardens. The villa, with its staggering bay and sea views, was in fact conceived by Beatrice de Rothschild as a setting for small-scale 18th-century musical soirées rather than as a home. www.azurialopera.com

STAY & EAT: the Grand-Hotel du Cap-Ferrat has an unrivalled location on the tip of the peninsula, a restaurant (Le Cap), a heated seawater pool and private seaside cabins. www.grand-hotel-cap-ferrat.com

ROSSINI FESTIVAL

Also held in August, the Pesaro Festival – as it is known to many performers after its host town, Giacomo Rossini's birthplace – was set up in 1980 to raise global awareness of some of the lesser known of his 35 or so operas. Many have since become part of the standard operatic repertoire. Pesaro is on the eastern coast of Italy, in the region of Le Marche. Operas are performed in the Adriatic Arena, the more intimate Teatro Rossini and the relatively recent (and smaller still) Teatro Sperimentale, where the emphasis is on obscure works by Rossini's contemporaries such as Coccia, Generali and Mosca. www.rossinioperafestival.it

STAY & EAT: not far north of Pesaro in Emilia-Romagna, Rimini's Grand Hotel was immortalised by Fellini in some of his films. There's also a spa on the private beach in summer. www.grandhotelrimini.com

Glastonbury

The world's biggest greenfield music and performing arts festival brings thousands of revellers flooding to the lovely Vale of Avalon with its age-old myths and religious traditions.

Set up in 1970 by a dairy farmer inspired by a blues festival, and featuring Marc Bolan in its first year, this most famous of music festivals began with an attendance of 1,500, and now welcomes 100 times that number. It's held over a 900-acre farming site in south-west England, amidst countryside variously claimed to be the place where King Arthur is buried, where Joseph of Arimathea walked and where several leylines converge. At the top of the site is the Sacred Space, a modern stone circle where revellers go at dawn to chant and play drums. Often accompanied by rain and mud, the festival is highly supportive of green issues, with some of the profits going to charitable causes.

It is held over a long weekend in June, and a variety of tastes are catered for: the Pyramid, Other and Dance stages feel like London nightclubs; the Acoustic area and Jazzworld are mellow and laid-back; the Field of Avalon, Tipi Field and Green Fields are more 'alternative'; and the Kidz Field and Theatre and Circus fields are family-oriented. As well as contemporary music, there's comedy, theatre, cabaret, circus and dance.

STAY

There are fields for camping all around the site; arrive early to secure a spot within your preferred zone. Popular areas are Pennard Hill Ground and The Park, Limekilns and Hitchin Hill Ground (both quieter spots), and Cockmill Meadow (for families). Alternatively, tipis can be booked in advance, or there are off-site options, including neighbouring Camp Kerala with its luxury tents.

If you prefer a hotel, towards Bath you'll find Babington House, the luxury outpost of London's Soho House private members' club, with a cinema, two restaurants, a spa, indoor and outdoor pools, tennis courts, a croquet lawn, a cricket pitch and a crèche.
www.babingtonhouse.co.uk

"Glastonbury Festival
is a midsummer celebration
of life and joy…"

Michael Eavis (founder)

Summer Music Festivals

Come rain or shine, the great British summer offers an impressive array of exciting festivals, some large-scale affairs featuring international acts, others more eccentric and intimate.

ISLE OF WIGHT FESTIVAL

The winner of the 'Best Major Festival' at the UK Festival Awards 2007, this mid-June weekender hosts headliners as big as The Police, The Rolling Stones and David Bowie for an audience of more than 60,000. It celebrated its tenth anniversary in 2008: although it began in 1968 and is now annual, there was a long hiatus until 2002 after unexpected overcrowding in 1970. Today it's held at the Seaclose Park recreation ground on the outskirts of Newport.
www.isleofwightfestival.com

WIRELESS FESTIVAL

The O2 Wireless Festival began in 2005 in London's Hyde Park, and though it subsequently extended to a second venue in Leeds, it dropped the latter in 2008 in favour of a series of pre-festival gigs around the UK in May and June. The festival itself takes place over four days in mid-June and features bands such as Fatboy Slim and Counting Crows as headline acts. Day and weekend tickets are available, including VIP packages.
www.o2wirelessfestival.co.uk

BIG CHILL

This decade-old multimedia festival bills itself as a celebration of music, art, dance and film but, above all, of life. More laid-back and intimate than Glastonbury, it is held over one weekend in late July/early August in the grounds of Eastnor Castle in Herefordshire – woods, lakes and an arboretum are set against the beautiful backdrop of the Malvern Hills. In addition to live performances (including classical music), there's a Body and Soul Area offering massages and treatments, a children's area, workshops, a late-night outdoor cinema, a comedy tent, a Victorian funfair and a playground in the family campsite. As an alternative to bringing a tent, you can pre-book tipis and Podpads (wooden huts). www.bigchill.net

SECRET GARDEN PARTY

This independent music festival is held over a long weekend in July or August within the grounds of a Georgian farmhouse near Huntingdon, with landscaped gardens and a lake and river. It is on a much smaller scale than most of the summer's offerings. The emphasis is on the quirky and the eclectic, in terms of both musical performances (reggae, rock, funk, hip hop, dub, dance and more, with DJs playing from a treehouse stage), the storytelling, theatre, comedy and art installations, and the activities on offer, which include snail racing, rubber duck shooting and Space Hopper races. The Sanctuary offers massage, healing, dance classes, yoga, saunas and hot tubs, and camping is available in tents, campers or caravans; alternatively, pre-book 'boutique' tipis or safari tents.
www.secretgardenparty.com

BESTIVAL

This self-described 'boutique music festival' takes place over three days on the Isle of Wight, at the Robin Hill Country Park near Newport. Set up in 2004 by leftfield Radio 1 DJ Rob da Bank and held each September, it focuses on pioneering music and on discovery, from its Bollywood Cocktail Bar, mass fancy dress party and Hidden Disco to its 'boutique campsite' with bivouacs, tipis, yurts and Podpads. www.bestival.net

"Life is a festival only to the wise."

Ralph Waldo Emerson

Royal Academy
Summer Exhibition

A long-standing favourite of the London art year, the Summer Exhibition sees members of the fêted Royal Academy compete against unknown artists to have their work displayed.

"The aim of art is to represent not the outward appearance of things, but their inward significance."

Aristotle

Founded in 1768 as a rival to the Society of Artists, the Royal Academy on London's Piccadilly has hosted its annual Summer Exhibition – the world's biggest open contemporary art exhibition – since its inception. The works are chosen from more than 11,000 entries by a rotating committee made up of practising artists. The submissions are paraded in front of committee members by a human chain of art-handlers; any work receiving the vote of more than three academicians passes through to the next round of selections.

More than 150,000 visitors a year come to admire around 1,200 works by established and unknown living artists, including paintings, sculpture, prints and architectural models. The event is held in the Academy's Main Galleries from June to August, with most works available to purchase.

STAY: the Athenaeum on Piccadilly has luxurious rooms, suites and apartments, many overlooking Green Park, plus a spa.
EAT: The Wolseley, also on Piccadilly, is a café-restaurant in the grand European tradition. It is an elegant place for breakfasts, pastries, afternoon teas, seafood and more.
www.athenaeumhotel.com;
www.thewolseley.com

OTHER LONDON GALLERIES
Somerset House
This neoclassical building at the end of The Strand was transformed into a centre for the visual arts in the late 20th century. It is home to The Courtauld Gallery, with its Old Master and Impressionist paintings, the Gilbert Collection of decorative arts, the Hermitage Rooms, hosting exhibitions of pieces loaned by St Petersburg's Hermitage Museum, and the Embankment Galleries, focusing on photography, design, fashion and architecture.
www.somersethouse.org.uk

National Gallery
Overlooking Trafalgar Square, this is one of the world's foremost collections of Western European painting. Dating back to the government's purchase of a private collection in 1824, the art is owned by the public and is free to view. www.nationalgallery.org.uk

Wallace Collection
Situated in an historic townhouse just off Oxford Street, this is a treasure trove of 18th-century French paintings, furniture and porcelain, and Old Master paintings.
www.wallacecollection.org

Bordeaux Fête le Vin

Bordeaux's summer festival offers a feast of food, wine and culture, in a region boasting the world's finest vineyards.

Held over four days in June since its debut in 2003, Bordeaux Fête le Vin ('Bordeaux Celebrates Wine') takes over the city's main square and waterside, offering wine tasting from the Aquitaine region (of which Bordeaux is capital), plus workshops, literary events, competitions, parades, banquets, concerts, fireworks and stalls selling regional foods.

The area around Bordeaux has roughly 9,000 wine-producing châteaux, 120,000 hectares of vineyards and 55 appellations. More than 700 million bottles are produced each year, from humble table wine to some of the world's most prized vintages, including premier cru reds from Médoc and Graves (Château Lafit-Rothschild, Château Margaux, Château Latour, Château Haut-Brion and Château Mouton-Rothschild).

Festival-goers can also purchase Vineyard Passes entitling them to tour local vineyard estates. Bilingual guides are on hand to explain all aspects of wine production.

STAY & EAT

Les Sources de Caudalie. This charming hotel south-west of Bordeaux boasts a Vinothérapie spa with wine-based treatments, plus a pool, golf course, two restaurants, a wine bar and even a cigar club in a tower with vineyard views. www.sources-caudalie.com

Within Bordeaux itself, La Maison Bord'eaux ('House by the Water') is a contemporary boutique hotel run by a member of a famous winegrowing family and offering fine cuisine, a wine bar, private cellar visits and château dinners. www.lamaisonbord-eaux.com

Explore: *the wine region*

Information on the following sites and the châteaux that can be visited is available from the Maisons de Vin at St-Emilion, Montagne, Côtes de Castillon and Fronsac.

BORDEAUX
- Your starting and finishing point.

ST-EMILION
- The first stop is known as 'the hill of a thousand wines' but is also famous for its Romanesque monolithic church and catacombs and its well-preserved medieval centre, now a UNESCO World Heritage Site.

ST-GEORGES, MONTAGNE AND LUSSAC
- It's worth making a detour along the country roads between these satellites of St-Emilion, which are lined with Romanesque churches and restored wine châteaux.

POMEROL
- On the way back towards Bordeaux, this village and small wine-growing region boasts lovely views from the hilly vineyards of the Côtes de Castillon and Côtes de Francs.

LIBOURNE
- The wine capital of the northern Gironde has a restored Gothic church, a 14th-century clock tower and a 16th-century town hall with a museum, and hosts a large food market at weekends.

FRONSAC
- This region produces very good reds and offers wonderful panoramic views from the town heights.

SUMMER

Bordeaux | St-Emilion | St-Georges | Pomerol | Libourne | Fronsac

Goodwood
Festival of Speed

A highlight of the motorsports calendar that attracts more than 150,000 people, Goodwood's festival celebrates competition cars and legendary drivers from the 19th century to today.

The Ascot of the motor racing world, dubbed 'the garden party of the Gods', takes place in mid-July in the scenic parkland surrounding Goodwood Park in West Sussex. Home to the Dukes of Richmond for more than three centuries and housing a renowned collection of paintings, porcelain and furniture, the estate is also famous as a horse-racing venue (see pp.104–5). It first saw hill-climbing and timed uphill sprints (often in vintage cars) in 1936, introduced by the 9th Duke. In 1993 his grandson, the current Earl of March, brought motorsports back to Goodwood in the form of a three-day hill climb and general celebration of car culture.

Motoring aficionados can, in addition to the hill climb, watch a 2.5-km (1.5-mile) loose-surface rally stage featuring around 30 historic vehicles, visit the Technology Pavilion with its displays on developments by car designers and manufacturers, and try out driving simulators and 4x4 driving. The lawns of the house, given over to the elegant and innovative entrants in the Cartier 'Style et Luxe' design award, are a civilised place for a picnic, or there are numerous food outlets around the site, including Green's Restaurant offering seafood and champagne.

STAY & EAT: Goodwood has its own hotel, The Goodwood Park Hotel, with characterful rooms, two restaurants, tennis courts, a spa and an indoor pool.
www.thegoodwoodparkhotel.co.uk

SUMMER

"Speed provides the one genuinely modern pleasure."

Aldous Huxley

Henley Royal Regatta

Presided over – and often attended by – the Royal Family, Henley's prestigious annual regatta attracts international crews and even Olympic champions, making it a must-see event in the sporting calendar.

The south Oxfordshire town of Henley-on-Thames is the setting for one of the world's most prestigious rowing events, held over five days (Wednesday to Sunday) that include the first weekend in July. Dating back to 1839, when it was put on by the mayor and townspeople as part of a fair, it now consists of head-to-head knockout races over a one-mile 550-yard (2.11-km) course (112 m longer than the international standard). The most long-standing, and prestigious, race is the Grand Challenge Cup for Men's Eights, awarded since the regatta's inception and open to all established amateur male crews.

Races can be watched by the general public from various points along the Berkshire (towpath) side of the Thames. The Stewards' Enclosure, at the end of the course and the

"A reach away the breach is made By dive and shout That circles out To Henley tower and town…"

Sir John Betjeman

location for the awards ceremony on the final day, is limited in access to the Stewards (former rowers who organise the regatta), and members of the enclosure and their guests; the waiting list for membership is years-long. The enclosure has covered grandstands, a bandstand, a marquee with a restaurant, bars and rolling lawns, and strictly enforces a dress code. The Regatta Enclosure just downstream is open to all by admission fee, as is Remenham Farm on both sides of the river at the first half of the course.

THE MUSEUM

Henley's River & Rowing Museum has permanent exhibitions on the town and its history, the River Thames and international rowing. The museum also boasts the country's only dedicated exhibition on *The Wind in the Willows*, the much loved book by Kenneth Grahame, which was inspired by the banks of the River Thames. Illustrator E.H. Shepard wandered the riverside at nearby Pangbourne, looking for inspiration. www.rrm.co.uk

STAY

East of Henley at Taplow near Maidenhead, the stately home hotel Cliveden, notorious for its role in the Profumo affair, boasts wonderful National Trust gardens and parkland, extravagant interiors, a spa, and indoor and outdoor pools.

In Henley itself, there's a member of the award-winning Hotel du Vin chain. www.clivedenhouse.co.uk; www.hotelduvin.com

Country Fairs

Lovers of all things rural can choose from a summer-long array of fairs featuring everything from farming and floral displays to extreme sports.

CLA GAME FAIR

In 2008 the biggest countryside exhibition in the world, the Country Land & Business Association Fair, celebrated its 50th year, offering a vast range of country sports and rural activities over three days in late July. The prestigious venues vary, but the event returns to Oxfordshire's Blenheim Palace, a UNESCO World Heritage Site and the birthplace of Winston Churchill, every four years.

As well as nearly 100 exhibitors, in areas such as Gunmaker's Row, Fisherman's Village, Gamekeeper's/Estate Management Row, the Regional Food Village and Elegant Gardens, there are various show spaces hosting demonstrations (cookery, fishing and more), displays (from falconry to ferret racing), debates and discussions, competitions, workshops and opportunities to 'Have a Go'. Activities include driving on a 4x4 course, field archery, caterpaulting, clay pigeon shooting and bungee trampolining. Parents can take advantage of a crèche for younger children. www.cla.org.uk

THE ROYAL SHOW

Organised by the Royal Agricultural Society of England and dating back to 1840, this four-day country show and fair held in Stoneleigh Park

in Warwickshire in early July promotes British farming within a framework of family-oriented entertainment. As well as livestock and horse competitions, there are show gardens, flower displays, a range of countryside pursuits and a Grand Ring hosting shows throughout the event. Food and drink stalls and trade stands complete the picture. More recently, there has been an Energy and Sustainability Park, a farmers' market, a Heavy Horse Area (with demonstration ring), and a Game & Country Skills section, with demonstrations and advice on everything from mole-catching to bow-making. www.royalshow.org.uk

OTHER ROYAL SHOWS
The Royal Bath & West Show
This four-day event, held in Somerset in late May, offers agricultural shows and events, rural craft shows, motorcycle displays and extreme sports. Popular attractions include show-jumping, heavy horses, steam engines, the cheese pavilion, craft stalls, the floral marquee and the interactive Eco-Zone. Visitors can also canoe on the lake, ride a mini railway and follow a Family Trail. www.bathandwest.com

The Royal Cornwall Show
Taking place over three days in early June at the Royal Cornwall Showground in Wadebridge, this show offers entertainments and activities such as a steam fair, flower show, livestock and rare breeds displays, showjumping, trade stands, local produce and crafts. www.royalcornwallshow.org

The Royal Highland Show
Spread over four days in mid-June at the Royal Highland Centre in Edinburgh, the show features almost 2,000 livestock exhibitors and competitors appearing from all over the British Isles. As well as beef and dairy cattle, there's almost every sheep breed native to the UK, dairy goats, and horses and ponies, including the three main native equine breeds. At the Rural Crafts Marquee, you can learn about bagpipe making, saddlery and willow-weaving. Music includes an appearance by the Highland Band Pipes and Drums. www.royalhighlandshow.org

The Royal Norfolk Show
The country's biggest two-day agricultural show is held at the Norfolk Showground in Norwich in late June, and includes sheep shows with shearing displays, and farriery demonstrations. www.royalnorfolkshow.co.uk

The Royal Lancashire Agricultural Show
This is the country's oldest, dating back to 1767, and it's hosted, as of 2008, in a new purpose-built home within the Duke of Lancaster Park at Barton. Held over three days in mid-July, it showcases agriculture, country crafts (cheese, honey and stick dressing – making shepherd's crooks and walking sticks), horses and horticulture. There are more than 200 trade stands, plus a riverbank fishing centre demonstrating angling techniques. www.rlas.co.uk

The Royal Welsh Show
In late July comes the Royal Welsh Showground at Llanelwedd in mid-Wales, celebrating local farming and rural life over four days with a variety of events, including carriage driving, mounted games, a parade of hounds, trotting and a display of vintage machinery. www.rwas.co.uk

The Egham Royal Show
Held over two days in late August, close to Runnymede about 40 minutes west of London, this show is 150 years old. Founded to encourage local farmers and labourers, it features a giant horticultural marquee, floral competitions, crafts, steam and traction engines, a vintage car display, and Punch and Judy shows. www.eghamroyalshow.org.uk

The Royal County of Berkshire Show
This two-day event, held in mid-September at Newbury Showground, celebrates the region's farming and rural communities with agricultural and countryside stands, a harvest festival service, a countryside pageant, a show garden, coaching parades, heavy horse displays, scurry racing (ponies 'scurrying' around a twisting course) and showjumping. www.newburyshow.co.uk

Pamplona's Running of the Bulls

The narrow cobbled streets of Pamplona's old town are the setting for one of the most exhilarating – and deadly – festival events in the world.

The *encierro* – or Running of the Bulls – is the most famous event in the Fiesta of San Fermin, held each July in the northern Spanish town of Pamplona. It began in the mid-1800s, when runners would herd bulls from corrals on the edge of town to the bullring for the afternoon's *corrida*. Today, anyone is allowed to join in this highly dangerous event, in which 14 people have been killed since 1924 and 200–300 are injured every year.

The running takes place at eight o'clock on eight consecutive mornings, taking an average of four minutes over a distance of 848 metres (half a mile). Spectators are protected by double barriers along the route (double so that runners can jump over the first fence if necessary). To get a good view at street level, you need to stake out a place by the outer barrier at least 90 minutes before the start; otherwise, locals rent out their balconies (20–30 euros a day). Within the bullring, the open terrace is free except at weekends, when it's 5 euros; a tier or upper tier costs 4 euros (5 at weekends). Firecrackers are set off when the bulls are freed into the streets and once they have been led into their pens in the bullring.

The Fiesta, or *Sanfermines*, which dates back to medieval times, opens with music and fireworks at noon on 7 July and closes at midnight on 14 July with a candlelit rendition of Pobre de Mí ('Poor Me'). In-between are a variety of traditional events honouring St Fermin, a funfair, and general revelry involving lots of sangria – at night the town becomes one big party. The first day is the best: an effigy of the saint is carried through the streets, accompanied by huge puppets, plus dancers and street entertainers.

"Everything became unreal...
and it seemed as though nothing
could have any consequences.
It seemed out of place to think of
consequences during the fiesta."

Ernest Hemingway

STAY

The town's one five-star option, the Gran
Hotel La Perla, has welcomed guests as
illustrious as Ernest Hemingway, Charlie
Chaplin and Orson Welles. Despite
recent renovation and the addition of
a new restaurant, it retains its old world
charm. www.granhotellaperla.com

Bastille Day

Vive la Révolution! Celebrations marking the biggest turning point in French history make for a riotously colourful spectacle in Paris.

Celebrations take place all over France on 14 July, commemorating the 1789 storming and surrender of the Bastille fortress and prison in Paris, which led ultimately to the Revolution and the abolition of the country's monarchy. The events in Paris are, unsurprisingly, the most fervent and spectacular. Crowds flock to the Champs-Elysées in the morning to watch a military parade led by the President and accompanied by policemen, firefighters and a display of jets flying over the Arc de Triomphe, leaving red, white and blue trails – the colours of the French tricolore flag. Amidst a street-party atmosphere that lasts all day, the crowds move on, to converge again by the Eiffel Tower to watch a stupendous hour-long firework display, accompanied by music and *son et lumière* effects, in the late evening.

But events kick off on the night of 13 July, when each arrondissement (district) hosts a 'bal des pompiers' ('firemen's ball'), a street party with live music and drinking. One of the best is in Place de la Contrescarpe in the 5th.

Many Métro stations are closed on the 14th, a national holiday, so set out early to find a good vantage point.

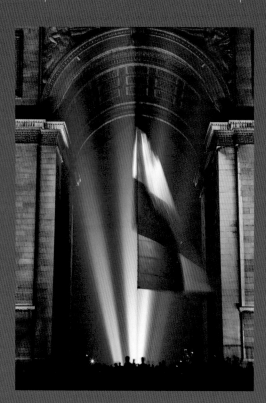

STAY
Just off the Champs-Elysées, the Hôtel Fouquet's Barrière is a chic option with two restaurants, a tea-room, and a spa with a pool.
www.lucienbarriere.com

EAT
Handy for the Eiffel Tower, both Pierre Gagnaire in the 8th and L'Astrance in the 16th have won awards for their world famous, innovative takes on French cuisine. Both require bookings weeks in advance.
www.pierre-gagnaire.com
L'Astrance, 4 rue Beethoven,
+33 (0)1 40 50 84 40.

"Head after head, and never heads enough. For those that bade them fall."

William Wordsworth

Killarney Races

Killarney's summer festival, one of the biggest events in the horse-racing calendar, draws fans from around the globe to the most idyllic of landscapes in south-west Ireland.

Drive: *the Ring of Kerry*

Blending spectacular landscapes, some of Europe's best beaches and many of Irelands's most fascinating remains (from Iron Age forts to stones with Ogham script to ancient monasteries), this 170-km (106-mile) tourist trail gets busy in summer. To enjoy the open roads, drive clockwise to avoid getting stuck behind the tour buses travelling anti-clockwise.

KILLARNEY
○ Your starting and finishing point.

KILLARNEY NATIONAL PARK
○ Next to the town, Ireland's first National Park is home to 15th-century Ross Castle, ancestral home of the O'Donoghue clan on the banks of Lough Leane. Another popular stopping point in the park is Ladies View, with wonderful lake and valley vistas. Muckross Estate, which can be visited, donated most of the money that enabled the National Park to come into being.

www.killarneysummerfest.com

Killarney's four-day races in mid-July, featuring entertainment for all the family and live music, have a festival atmosphere. Indeed, they are part of the Killarney Summerfest, which also hosts outdoor theatre and concerts, hot-air ballooning, art exhibitions and children's events. Racing – both national hunt and flat – takes place over three evenings, beginning just before 6pm, and the final day is devoted to fashion and a spa marquee.

The Summer Races began in 1947 and attract many famous faces. Killarney Racecourse, which dates back more than 175 years (70 at its current location), is seen by many as one of the world's most picturesque racecourses – Killarney and the nearby Ring of Kerry are well-known beauty spots, with stunning mountains, lakes and woods. The racecourse is on the banks of the Flesk river, a site frequented by the Fianna warriors more than two millennia ago.

STAY & EAT
The Aghadoe Heights in Killarney has lake views, a peaceful spa and indoor pool, tennis courts and eclectic European cuisine in its Lake Room restaurant. www.aghadoeheights.com

STAIGUE IRON AGE FORT
- This partially ruined round stone fort close to Sneem has been dated to AD 300–400, when it is believed, with its walls up to 4 metres (13 ft) thick, to have been a local lord or king's defensive stronghold, as well as a place of worship and an observatory.

DERRYNANE HOUSE
- Derrynane was home to Irish hero and people's rights crusader Daniel O'Connell, and at his former house you can see the gold chariot he rode through Dublin after his release from prison. His family graveyard is close by at Abbey Island. The area has wonderful clean beaches popular with surfers.

VALENTIA ISLAND, SAINT FINNANS BAY AND BALLINSKELLIGS
- Passing though Waterville, where Charlie Chaplin liked to take holidays (a fact commemorated by the statue of him there), you can make an excursion off the official Ring route to Valentia Island, accessible by ferry or over a bridge at Portmagee. This was the site of the first transatlantic telegraph cable linking Europe with America, and has a slate quarry, a lighthouse and therapod dinosaur footprints.

Portmagee is a picturesque fishing village, and a great centre for sea angling. From here there are views of the Skelligs, two steep rocky islands that are home to a UNESCO-listed early Christian monastery, as well as colonies of gannets and puffins.

The Open Golf

The only major men's golf
championship held outside the
USA provides a thrilling spectacle
over a rota of nine different courses.

"Golf, like the measles, should be
caught young, for, if postponed to riper
years, the results may be serious."

P.G. Wodehouse

The oldest of the world's four major men's championships was first played at Prestwick in Scotland in 1860, between eight players over three rounds of a 12-hole course. The Open is now administered by the R&A (the golf-world rules and development body) and is hosted on nine historic links courses in the United Kingdom. It takes place over four days, including the weekend of the third Friday in July, making it the third major of the year after The Masters and the US Open and before the PGA Championship.

Most of the 156 places are taken by top players who are exempt from qualifying, usually because they feature in the top 50 in the Official World Golf Rankings, have won one of the other majors, or are in the top 10 from the previous year's Open. In 2007 the prize money totalled £4.2 million, the highest of any of the majors.

The venue rota usually alternates between Scotland and England each year; every fifth year or so the Open is played at St Andrews, 'the Home of Golf' on the east coast of Scotland. St Andrews' Old Course hosts the Championship in 2010, its 150th anniversary.

2009 Westin Turnberry, Ayrshire
www.turnberry.co.uk

2010 St Andrews, Fife
www.standrews.org.uk

2011 Royal St George's, Sandwich, Kent
www.royalstgeorges.com

2012 Royal Lytham & St Annes,
Lancashire www.royallytham.org

STAY & EAT
The Westin Turnberry is a spectacular resort with links, a hotel, cottages and lodges, a spa, and three eateries. www.turnberry.co.uk

The Fairmont St Andrews has two golf courses of its own, a spa and an indoor pool. www.fairmont.com/standrews

Wallett's Court is a country house hotel, spa and restaurant in a Kentish Jacobean manor. www.wallettscourthotel.com

Big Blue Hotel, at Blackpool's Pleasure Beach, is chic, cool and contemporary. www.bigbluehotel.com

Il Palio Siena

The city's famous scallop-shaped Piazza del Campo is transformed into a racecourse as the bareback horserace is run, causing huge excitement among locals and visitors.

Run for the first time in 1721, the Palio is a historic pageant celebrating Siena's 17 *contrade* (districts), who race against each other; each of the jockeys and horses wear their *contrada*'s colours, and there is a parade in medieval costume around the Piazza before the race begins. Once the rope is dropped, the race is over in less than two minutes. The horses charge around the Piazza's narrow track three times at breakneck speed – unlike other races, a horse can win even if the jockey has fallen.

The standing area in the Piazza is free, but you must arrive very early to get a spot and once you are in, you'll be stuck in the heat for about four hours. Try to get a ticket for a seat in the terraces – apply early – or make some enquiries and book a space on a private balcony.

Explore: *south of Siena*

This is quintessential Tuscany – rolling wheat fields, cypresses and hilltop towns and farmhouses.

SIENA
- o The start and end point.

BUONCONVENTO
- o Don't miss the Sacred Art Museum.

MONTALCINO
- o This hilltop town boasts beautiful views over the Tuscan countryside. Sample some of the famous Brunello di Montalcio at Castello Banfi Vineyard Estate in nearby Sant'Angelo Scalo. Don't miss the isolated Romanesque Abbazia di Sant'Antimo a few kilometres south of the town.

SAN QUIRICO D'ORCIA
- o The Horti Leonini is a fine example of an Italian garden.

PIENZA
- o This is a rare example of a planned Renaissance model city.

MONTEPULCIANO
- o Tuscany's highest hill town, famous for its wine. Eat at nearby La Chiusa in Montefollonico and be sure to visit the 13th-century Abbazia di Monte Oliveto Maggiore.

Glorious Goodwood

The beautiful Sussex racecourse hosts one of the season's best-loved social and sporting events, described by King Edward VII as 'a garden party with racing tacked on' but offering world-class sport.

Sussex's Goodwood Park estate, which first saw horse-racing in 1802 under the 3rd Duke of Richmond, is even more famous for its flat racing than as a motorsports venue (see pp.88–89) – and for its chic summer fashions, comprising linen suits and Panama hats for men and classic styles for women.

The event, which lasts for five days in late July/early August, includes two of Britain's 31 Group One flat races, the Sussex Stakes and the Nassau Stakes.

The main Gordon Enclosure affords access to the Sussex Grandstand and the paddock, which includes the parade ring and winners' enclosure. There's also a restaurant serving afternoon tea and three-course meals. The Lennox Enclosure offers great

views of the horses as they gallop along the home straight; race-goers here can bring picnics, although snacks are available. The Richmond Enclosure, which affords access to the winners' enclosure and parade ring, is reserved for members and their guests and corporate clients. It has several restaurants, including the award-winning Charlton Hunt, facing the winning post and offering panoramic vistas taking in Chichester and the Isle of Wight, and The Double Trigger, serving local seafood. There's also a champagne bar.

www.goodwood.co.uk/horseracing

STAY

For the Goodwood Park Hotel, see p.89.
East of Chichester at Climping, the Bailiffscourt
Hotel & Spa was built in the 1920s. Peacocks
strut around on the extensive parkland, and
there are indoor and outdoor pools, tennis
courts and a croquet lawn. It is just a few
minutes' walk from Climping Beach.
www.hshotels.co.uk

"There is something about
the outside of a horse that
is good for the inside
of a man…"

Winston Churchill

Chatsworth
Country Fair

One of Britain's most famous historic houses, the 'Palace of the Peak' makes a fine venue for this lively celebration of the countryside.

The bank holiday weekend at the end of August sees the magnificent Chatsworth House in the Peak District, home to the Duke and Duchess of Devonshire, given over to a three-day outdoor event celebrating rural life. Among the offerings are hot-air balloon and parachuting displays, massed pipe and military bands, and more than 300 craft and trade stands. The Grand Ring hosts a vintage car parade, terrier and ferret racing and more, and there's a clay pigeon shoot, blacksmith's demonstration, archery and sheep-dog trials.

Throughout the fair, guests have access to Chatsworth House itself, built by Bess of Hardwick in the 16th century, to its superb collection of European art, and to its wonderful park and gardens with their stunning water features. The farm and adventure playground are closed but there's a bouncy castle and old-fashioned fairground for family fun.

106

STAY
You can stay on the estate itself, in the Duke's self-catering cottages, in guesthouses offered by estate tenants, or in the Cavendish Hotel on the park's fringes, with a restaurant and exclusive fishing for guests. Some of its superior rooms, mainly in the original 18th-century Peacock Inn, have four-posters and cast-iron fireplaces. www.cavendish-hotel.net

"Summer makes a silence after spring."

Vita Sackville-West

Explore: *a Peak District drive*

HATHERSAGE

○ North of Chatsworth, this is the site
where Robin Hood is said to have
hidden in a cave and where Little John,
one of his 'Merry Men', is reputed to be
buried. It also has connections with the
Brontës – it is widely accepted that *Jane
Eyre* was set here, following a visit by
Charlotte Brontë to the village in 1845.
The village is a popular spot, with views
over the Hope and Derwent valleys,
climbing and hill-walking opportunities,
and an all-year outdoor swimming pool
and café.

CASTLETON

○ West across the Hope Valley lies
Castleton, where a unique mineral,
Blue John, is mined: among the caverns
open to visitors are Speedwell, through
which you can take a boat trip. You can
also visit the ruined Peveril Castle with
its fabulous views.

EDALE

○ A detour to the west takes you to the
starting point of the Pennine Way, the
long-distance footpath that stretches
all the way to Scotland.

DERWENT RESERVOIR

○ It's at the Derwent Dam that the
'Dambusters' rehearsed their daring
low-level raids on the Ruhr Valley in
Germany, in 1943, and here that the
subsequent film was shot.

SNAKE PASS

○ This famous stretch of winding road,
the highest section of the A37 between
Sheffield and Manchester (the part
between Ladybower Reservoir and
Glossop), affords incredible views
over the Peak District and Manchester.

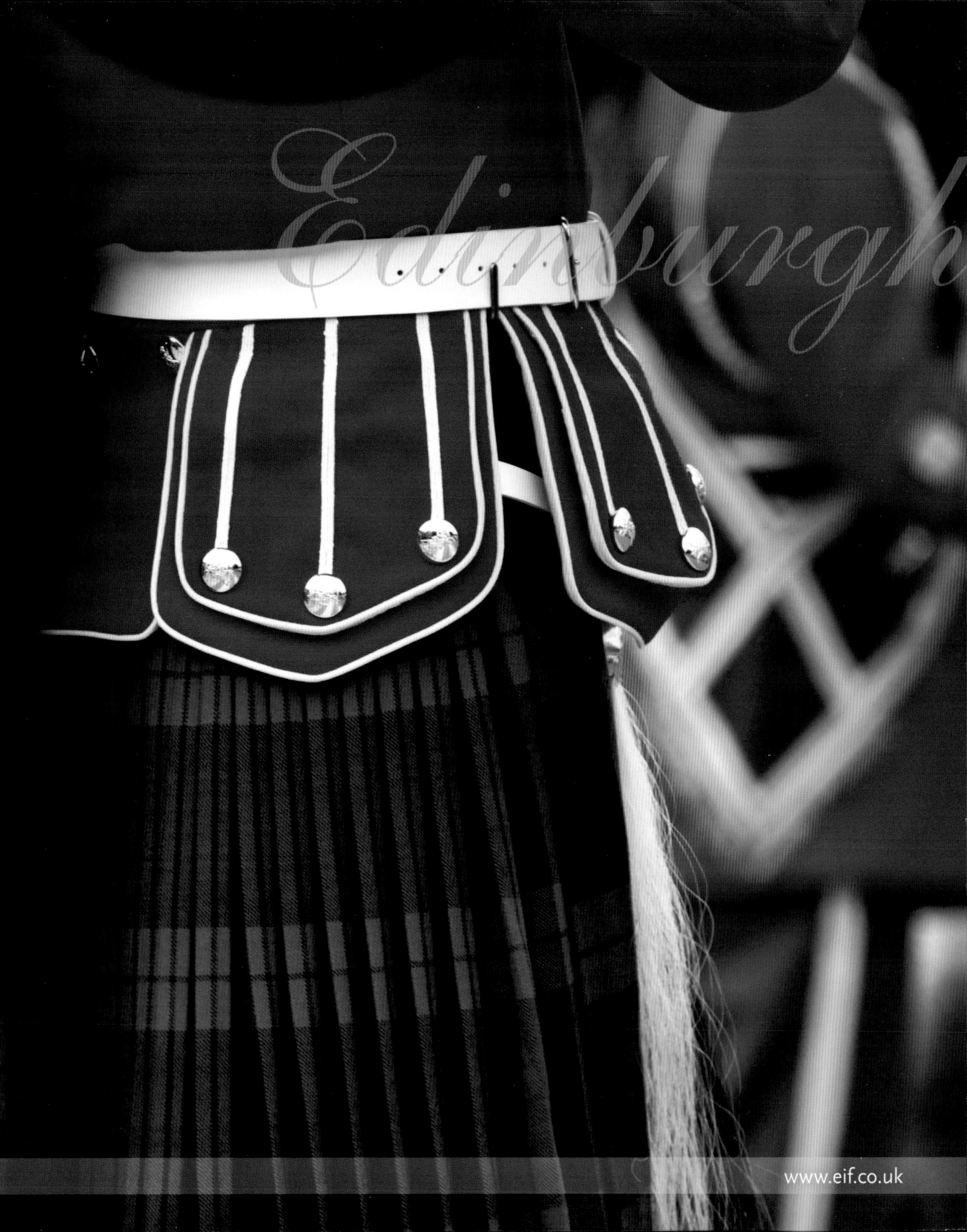
Edinburgh
www.eif.co.uk

Edinburgh
International Festival

This 'platform for the flowering of the human spirit' brings a profusion of classical music, theatre, opera and dance talent from around the world to Scotland's capital.

The Edinburgh International Festival, which celebrated its 60th anniversary in 2007, has given rise to around ten associated festivals that are together known as the 'Edinburgh Festival'.

It differs from the Edinburgh Fringe – the first festival to have been inspired by it – in that participation is by invitation, whereas the Fringe has no selection process. Other events include the Military Tattoo and Book, Film, Jazz and Mela festivals in July and August, plus, at other times of the year, the Hogmanay Festival (see pp.168–9) and the Science and Children's Festivals.

The International Festival was set up with the aim of enriching the cultural life of Scotland, Britain and Europe as a whole, by a committee including Rudolf Bing, then general manager of Glyndebourne Opera

(see pp.36–37) and the festival's first director. This three-week-long fest from August to early September focuses on the performing arts (classical music, theatre, opera and dance). Since 1999 the festival has had a year-round home at The Hub, Edinburgh's Festival Centre, a listed building with an impressive spire, featuring contemporary sculptures and stained glass.

The Fringe is the world's largest arts festival, featuring over 18,000 performers and selling over 1.6 million tickets a year. It is an exuberant celebration of every kind of performing art from dance and theatre to mime, street theatre and comedy. Every possible performance space in Edinburgh is taken over for the festival; visitors can enjoy round-the-clock performances and revel in the non-stop party atmosphere.

SUMMER

STAY & EAT
The Balmoral has a Michelin-starred restaurant, an award-winning spa, sumptuous rooms and suites with décor inspired by the Scottish landscape, and views of the castle, the old town or the hotel's internal courtyard.

Restaurant Martin Wishart in Leith, Edinburgh's regenerated port, is globally renowned for its French cooking, both traditional and modern.
www.thebalmoralhotel.com
www.martin-wishart.co.uk

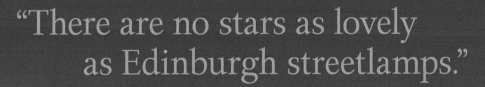

"There are no stars as lovely as Edinburgh streetlamps."

Robert Louis Stevenson

Cowes Week

Traditionally held between Glorious Goodwood and the Glorious Twelfth, the annual Isle of Wight regatta has long been a magnet for royalty, the nobility and the rich and famous.

One of the UK's longest-running sporting events, Cowes Week has been a highlight of the social calendar since 1827 (its second year), when George IV showed his approval of the previous year's seven-yacht race, held under the flag of the Royal Yacht Club, by presenting the King's Cup. Now extended to eight days in early August, it stages up to 40 daily races for more than 1,000 boats in nearly forty handicap, one-design and multihull classes, and in the process offers a unique mix of classic and state-of-the-art designs.

The 8,500 or so competitors range from weekend sailors to world-class and Olympic yachtsmen and -women, while a crowd of more than 100,000 enjoy a festival atmosphere climaxing in a fabulous firework display on the final Friday. Parties and live street entertainment are focused on Cowes Parade, which has a central information point, stands offering free introductory sailing sessions, a landing from which spectator boat services depart, great views of the starting lines, and a bar and barbecue overlooking the Solent. Alternatively, Cowes Yacht Haven, open to professionals, amateurs and spectators by ticket, has a waterside port and champagne bar, a beer tent, food and trade stalls, and a live entertainment stage. Events here include a ball and the prize-giving ceremony on the last Saturday.

> **STAY**
> At Ventnor, known as 'the Madeira of England', the Royal Hotel has comfortable rooms, an award-winning restaurant, a garden with tropical plants and pool, and coastal, southerly views.
> www.royalhoteliow.co.uk

"A smooth sea never made a skilled mariner."

English proverb

Drive:
the Island

ALUM BAY
○ Drive west via Yarmouth to reach this sandy bay with its famous multi-coloured cliffs. There are spectacular views of The Needles, a row of three chalk stacks that rise out of the sea, with a lighthouse at the western end, and a chair-lift down to the beach. In the area you'll find restaurants and a picnic spot.

BLACKGANG CHINE
○ Head south to Ventnor and this dramatic natural chine (coastal ravine) nearby. Blackgang is also home to the UK's oldest theme park, and is a good place for coastal walks affording views over the Channel. Many dinosaur fossils have been found here.

SHANKLIN
○ East of Blackgang, Shanklin is also a stopping point for its chine, as well as its Old Village with thatched cottages and shops selling traditional crafts, and its cliff-lift to the seafront.

RYDE OR FISHBOURNE
○ Ferries back to the mainland depart from these towns.

UK Regattas

The south-west coast is the setting for some of the summer's most festive sailing events, bringing together yachts, historic craft, working boats, and a variety of displays, funfairs, music, markets and other entertainments.

DARTMOUTH ROYAL REGATTA

The Port of Dartmouth Royal Regatta in South Devon, which takes place over three days in late August (from the last Wednesday to the last Friday of the month), is a water-based extravaganza of rowing, displays of historic craft, river tug-of-war, yacht racing and traditional passage races. But there's more besides: air displays (usually featuring the Red Arrows) and two stunning firework displays, while the town is transformed by a funfair, music, dancing, and market stalls and a shopping village.

For centuries, sailors have set out all over the world from Dartmouth's deep-water harbour, which is surrounded by steep hillsides packed with brightly coloured houses. Dartmouth first hosted a regatta in 1822, with royal patronage coming in 1856 after Queen Victoria made a chance visit due to bad weather. It's now patronised by HRH the Duke of York, who trained at the town's naval college, and the regatta always has one naval guard-ship in the harbour.

The official opening ceremony traditionally takes place on a Wednesday. It features a procession led by the band of Her Majesty's Royal Marines from the college, who then 'Beat Retreat' – a tradition dating back to medieval battles, when a drummer boy would be sent along the infantry ranks, his drumming telling the soldiers to retire to their overnight quarters or garrison.
www.dartmouthregatta.co.uk
STAY: the Dart Marina Hotel comprises stylish rooms, suites and apartments, a restaurant and a bistro, and Dartmouth's only luxury spa, including an exercise pool.
www.dartmarinahotel.com

FOWEY ROYAL REGATTA

Part of the Fowey Carnival, this royal regatta – which usually takes place in the southern Cornish town over the third full week of August – is among the country's best local regattas, with a family ambience. Over the years it has been visited by Queen Victoria and Queen Elizabeth. As well as sailing (including a quirky raft race and the Falmouth Working Boats race), it features a display by the Red Arrows, carnival processions, live music, children's entertainment, a giant Cornish pasty ceremony, crab-catching and fireworks over the harbour.
www.foweyroyalregatta.co.uk
STAY & EAT: Fowey Hall Hotel & Restaurant occupies a Cornish mansion with stunning views over the estuary and sea below, a spa and pool opened in 2008, a supervised children's 'den' and excellent cuisine based on local seafood. www.foweyhallhotel.co.uk

Also boasting sea and river views, the boutique Marina Villa Hotel mixes contemporary luxe with original character, and is home to the Michelin-starred Restaurant Nathan Outlaw.
www.themarinahotel.co.uk

"…whatever we lose
(like a you or a me)
it's always ourselves
we find in the sea."

E.E. Cummings

113

OTHER REGATTAS

Swanage Regatta and Carnival, Dorset
A week of nautical delights, culminating in a carnival
procession (July). www.swanagecarnival.com

Port of Plymouth Regatta, Devon
Competitive racing for monohull yachts and dinghies
(July–August). www.plymouthregatta.com

Christchurch Regatta and Carnival, Dorset
An annual rowing regatta on the River Stour (August).
www.visitchristchurch.info

Torbay Royal Regatta, Devon
This regatta offers yacht racing, Skiffs National
Championship and evening entertainment (August).
www.torbayweek.co.uk

Falmouth Week Festival, Cornwall
An internationally recognised sailing regatta, dating from
the 1820s. Maritime events, including top level competitive
racing, are complemented by a full range of evening
entertainments (August).
www.falmouthweek.co.uk

La Tomatina

114

www.latomatina.es

There are no winners in Spain's unique battle of the tomatoes, but all of the 40,000 or so revellers come away happy.

On the last Wednesday in August, the otherwise quiet town of Buñol, close to Valencia on the east coast of Spain, becomes a riot of colour as people take to the streets to pelt one another with nearly 140 tons of over-ripe tomatoes brought in from the surrounding countryside. Of the various claims to the event's origin, the most likely theory is that it started as a class-war between local youths in the 1940s.

The night before the fight, wine and food flow, especially paella, the regional speciality, served in the Concurso des Paellas near the Plaza del Pueblo.

The fight, which takes place beneath the town's imposing medieval bell-tower, commences at 10am, at the firing of a rocket. Participants, who generally wear safety goggles and old T-shirts and shorts, have to squish the tomatoes before throwing them. After an hour, another rocket sounds to signal that it's time for fire-trucks to hose down the streets. However, the festival itself – held in honour of the town's patron saints – lasts a week, comprising a host of other events including parades, live music, dancing, food stalls, a paella-cooking contest and fireworks.

VALENCIA

Spain's third largest city brims with fascinating old buildings, including La Lonja, a Gothic silk exchange now listed as a UNESCO World Heritage Site, the Gothic cathedral and neighbouring Basilica of the Virgin, the Art Deco train station Estación del Norte, the Roman and Arabic structures of the Barrio del Carmen, and towers that once formed part of the city walls. But the modernist and modern buildings are as much of an attraction: they include the huge Mercado Central market and the futuristic City of Arts and Sciences, designed by native Valencian architect Santiago Calatrava, containing an opera house, science museum, sea-life centre, IMAX cinema and planetarium, restaurants and more. There are some very fine sandy beaches here too.

STAY & EAT
Accommodation is limited in Buñol, so most visitors stay in Valencia 40 km (25 miles) away. A five-star option in the city is the boutique Hospes Palau de la Mar in a stately 19th-century building, with a spa and indoor pool, a courtyard garden and a gourmet restaurant. www.hospes.es

"Everything being a constant carnival, there is no carnival left."

Victor Hugo

Bristol Balloon Fiesta

One of the biggest free outdoor spectacles in all of Europe provides gravity-defying displays of ballooning prowess from around the world.

Thirty years old in 2008, this superb hot-air ballooning festival is held over four days in August. It attracts up to half a million visitors to the lovely rolling parkland of the Ashton Court Estate in the West Country, complete with mansion, deer parks, woodlands, ancient oaks, golf courses, mountain-bike and walking trails and wonderful views over nearby Bristol.

Highlights of the free event are the mass ascents of 120 balloons at dawn and dusk, the Special Shapes Rodeo with its strangely or comically shaped balloons (among perennial favourites are the Churchill dog, the Kiwi bird and the Scottish Piper), the Night Glows, which combines lit-up balloons and fireworks with a musical soundtrack (so popular that there are now two) and 'Heaven', a special area providing carnivalesque entertainments. Other attractions are a display of model hot-air balloons from around Europe, children's activities, food and drink stalls, and trade stands. Note that if you want to actually ride in a hot-air balloon, you need to contact a balloon company in advance (Bailey Balloons 01275 375 300; Bristol Balloons 0117 963 7858; or First Flight 01934 852 875).

STAY & EAT: Hotel du Vin is a restored sugar warehouse in Bristol, with its own bistro. www.hotelduvin.com
Forty-eight km (30 miles) from Bristol, Whatley Manor is an intimate hotel in a converted Cotswolds manor, with sophisticated rooms, a cinema, an award-winning spa with a pool, a restaurant and a brasserie, and landscaped grounds. www.whatleymanor.com

OTHER ATTRACTIONS

Bristol Docks is home to Brunel's SS Great Britain, which has won numerous awards, and was recently voted 'UK Museum of the Year'. The world's first great ocean liner, it has faithfully re-created interiors, including the first-class dining saloon and steerage quarters. Beside the vessel is the departure point for harbour tours, some aboard a reconstruction of the Matthew, in which John Cabot is said to have 'discovered' America ahead of Columbus. www.ssgreatbritain.org; www.matthew.co.uk

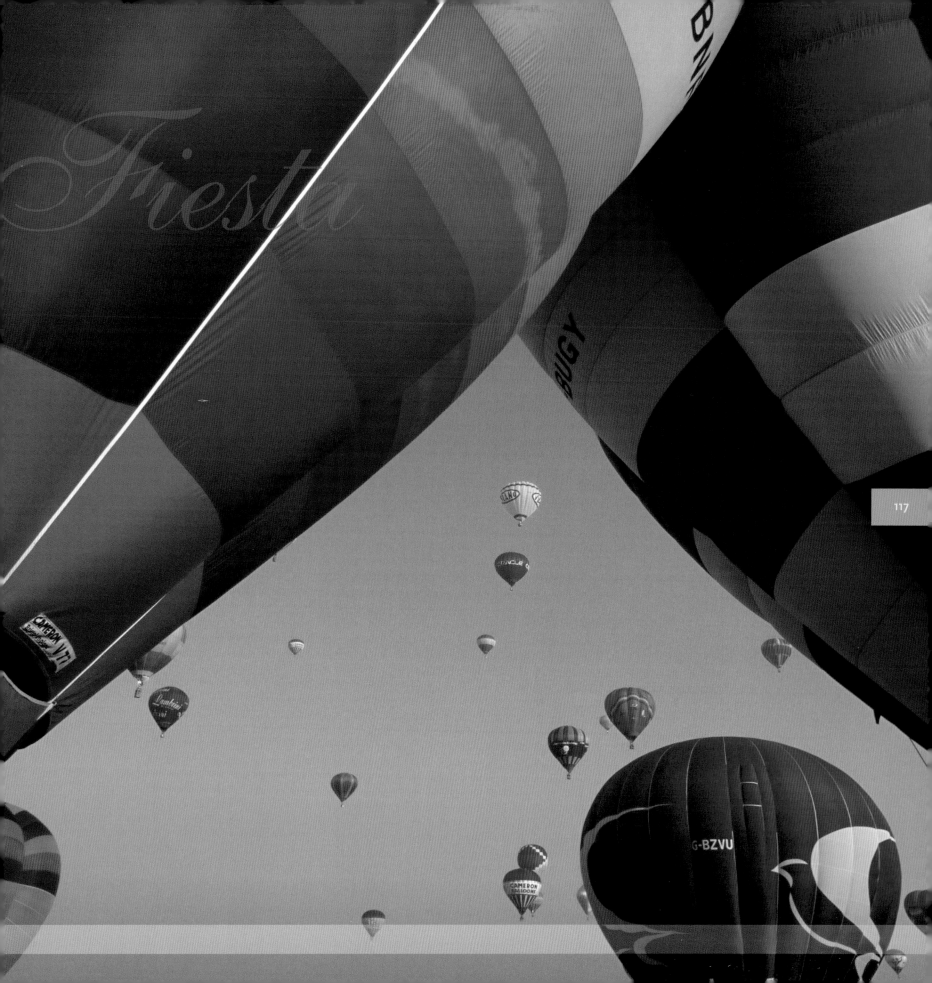

As the nights draw in and leaves turn copper, gold and russet, the autumn harvest is celebrated everywhere. A profusion of food festivals revel in seasonal produce – from apples to oysters and truffles – while beer and cider festivals mark the waning of the year. Falling temperatures relieve the lassitude of late summer, and golf and horse racing beckon. Victorian traditions are maintained with the pomp and circumstance of the Proms and the pageantry of the Highland Games. Spectacular fireworks light up the autumnal sky as Bonfire Night is celebrated.

Autumn

"It was Autumn,
and incessant
Piped the quails from
shocks and sheaves,
And, like living
coals, the apples
Burned among the
withering leaves…"

Henry Wadsworth Longfellow

Golf in Europe

Keen golfers and fans of the sport can enjoy the autumnal
season at a number of outstanding – and demanding –
courses around Europe.

LE GOLF NATIONAL (L'ALBATROS)

This course (6,600 m, par 71) at Guyancourt near Versailles to the west of Paris, about 32 km (20 miles) from the centre, has played host to June's French Open since 1990. It has innovative features that enable a large number of spectators to watch the players and follow the various stages of a game. It is considered a remarkable and very tough course that may one day host a Ryder Cup. www.golf-national.com www.opendefrance.fr
STAY & EAT: the sumptuous Trianon Palace & Spa in Versailles has two restaurants, one of which is presided over by Gordon Ramsay. www.starwoodhotels.com

CHANTILLY VINEUIL

Vineuil (6,396 m, par 71) in the Picardy & Oise region of northern France, just 45 km (30 miles) from Paris, is considered one of the finest and most challenging courses on the Continent. Designed in 1909, it has an attractive clubhouse and magnificent parkland setting. It now hosts the Championnat International de France, Coupe Louis Murat in May/June. Taking in the neighbouring Les Longères course (6,972 m, par 73), it has recently been upgraded from 18 to 36 holes. www.golfdechantilly.com; www.ffgolf.org
STAY & EAT: the Four Seasons Hôtel George V Paris, just off the Champs-Elysées, has many rooms and suites boasting private terraces and a Michelin-starred restaurant, Le Cinq. www.fourseasons.com/paris

LES BORDES

St Laurent Nouan in France's Loire Valley is home to this award-winning 18-hole woodland course (6,420 m, par 72), considered one of Europe's – perhaps even the world's – best and most taxing. It has Europe's biggest green, overlooked by an original Rodin statue, 12 water holes and a number of lakes dotted amidst the ancient oaks, firs and birches.
STAY & EAT: Les Bordes is a former hunting estate with its own accommodation in restored Loire cottages and farm buildings, and a dining room where you can enjoy authentic French cuisine and wines from local vineyards. www.lesbordes.com

ROYAL ZOUTE

Belgium's best course is on the North Sea near the Dutch border, in the resort of Knokke Le Zoute (Knokke-Heist) 25 km (15 miles) from Bruges. Set amidst a wild landscape of dunes and woods, and described by Nick Faldo as a 'hidden gem', it has the tricky Extérieur championship course (6,172 m, par 72) and the Intérieur executive course (par 64). British influence has always been strong here, with all the captains hailing from across the Channel since the club's inauguration in 1909. The Extérieur was several times host to the now-defunct Belgian Open. www.zoute.be
STAY & EAT: Knokke's Manoir du Dragon has stylish rooms melding traditional and more contemporary décor and lovely gardens; ask about two-night offers including dinner in a top local restaurant. www.manoirdudragon.be

KENNEMER GOLF & COUNTRY CLUB

This classic Dutch links course (6,216 m, par 72), about half an hour from Amsterdam in the popular seaside resort of Zandvoort, moved to its current location amidst the sand dunes in 1927. Since 1985 it has had 27 holes, divided into three nine-hole courses: the Van Hengel (A) and Harry Colt (C) courses follow the original layout and are considered the best. The atmospheric, refined clubhouse has a thatched roof. www.kennemergolf.nl; www.klmopen.nl
STAY & EAT: Duin & Kruidberg Country Estate in the Zuid Kennemerland National Park near Zandvoort is a prestigious castle-hotel with luxurious traditional rooms, two restaurants and a Finnish sauna. www.duin-kruidberg.nl

GUT LARCHENHOF

The only Jack Nicklaus-designed golf course in Germany, Gut Lärchenhof, near Cologne, was opened as recently as 1997; a year later the prestigious German masters moved there. The 220-m 8th is one of the longest par three holes in European golf. This club is the venue for the Mercedes-Benz Championship in mid-September, which features the top 75 players of the official World Golf rankings. The four-day event draws crowds of up to 60,000, and substantial television audiences worldwide. www.gutlaerchenhof.de
STAY & EAT: Just 12 km (8 miles) from Cologne city centre, the Grandhotel Schloss Bensberg is a 300-year-old Baroque castle with elegant modern decor, a spa and Michelin-starred French cuisine. www.schlossbensberg.com

Food Festivals
Wales and the Marches

September is a packed month for lovers of Welsh produce, with a number of excellent festivals celebrating locally-produced meat, cheese, wine and cider, and offering many gourmet experiences.

LUDLOW MARCHES FOOD & DRINK FESTIVAL

Held over a long weekend in mid-September, this Shropshire festival showcases more than 120 small independent food and drink producers from the Welsh Marches (border regions), offering everything from rare breeds of meat and gourmet sausages to real ale, cider and perry. Some 20,000 visitors come to the tented village within Ludlow's ruined medieval castle. Fun events include the famous Sausage Trail, the Cake Trail and the Pork Pie of the Marches competition.

In the mid-1990s, Ludlow began to be recognised as a centre of culinary excellence, with more Michelin-starred restaurants than anywhere outside London (two have since closed or relocated).
www.foodfestival.co.uk

STAY & EAT: Mr Underhill's is a Michelin-starred 'restaurant with rooms', with a lovely plant-filled courtyard. www.mr-underhills.co.uk

ABERGAVENNY

Abergavenny's festival – described by the *Observer Food Monthly* as 'the Glastonbury of food festivals' – also celebrates produce of the Marches, as well as places further afield, in mid-September.

Special areas are dedicated to cheese, local wines and fish, and local restaurants offer samples of 'street food' in the Market Hall. There are talks, debates, book signings, masterclasses and cookery demonstrations, tutored tastings, events for children, walks, appearances by foodie celebrities, live music in the castle and craft stalls.
www.abergavennyfoodfestival.com

STAY & EAT: Allt Yr Ynys Country House Hotel & Restaurant in nearby Walterstone is a 16th-century manor retaining many original features. It also has an indoor pool, an award-winning restaurant and walled garden with an Elizabethan knot garden.
www.allthotel.co.uk

MOLD FOOD & DRINK FESTIVAL

This festival in North Wales was set up by the Mold Hotel and Restaurant Association. It features demonstrations by celebrity chefs, local cooking competitions, farm shops and farmers' markets, honey, olives, oils, and more – the remit goes beyond the purely Welsh to include cuisine from as far afield as India. Local entertainers keep the mood lively and the crowds entertained throughout the weekend.

Mold is a foodie mecca throughout the year, with numerous delis, a street market on Wednesdays and Saturdays, and the Celyn Farmer's Market on the first Saturday of the month. www.moldfoodfestival.co.uk
STAY & EAT: Soughton Hall, an 18th-century bishop's palace in nearby Northop, boasts mullioned windows and Islamic turrets added by owner William John, a famous traveller. Guests can walk in the stunning private grounds and eat in the award-winning Stables Bar Restaurant. www.soughtonhall.co.uk

GREAT BRITISH CHEESE FESTIVAL

Held over a weekend in late September, this festival moved around each year after its inception in 2000 but finally found a permanent home at Cardiff Castle in South Wales in 2008. Describing itself as a mix of a royal picnic and a 'farmers' market with with attitude', it features, Britain's biggest cheese market (with nearly 200 stalls and 500 cheeses to sample and buy), but also offers masterclasses, workshops and demonstrations, whisky, beer, cider, perry and wine tastings, and a wealth of other products, from gourmet breads to prize-winning pies. The Festival even plays host to the World Cheese Tossing Finals.
www.thecheeseweb.com
STAY & EAT: Cardiff's best option is the St David's Hotel & Spa beside Mermaid Quay, in a modern building with a glass atrium. All rooms have sea-facing balconies, and there's a bar and grill offering Welsh specialities and an indoor pool and marine spa providing thalassotherapy treatments and more.
www.stdavidshotelcardiff.co.uk

"Dining is and always was a great artistic opportunity."

Frank Lloyd Wright

Food Festivals
England and Ireland

September and October see more foodie fun at some of the season's tastiest events. Gourmet adventures can be coupled with journeys of discovery in beautiful countryside.

ORGANIC FOOD FESTIVAL

Early September sees Europe's biggest celebration of the sustainable lifestyle when the Soil Association's food festival takes over Bristol's harbourside (Millennium Square, Anchor Square and the Amphitheatre area) for a weekend. Regular features are food and drink stalls, cookery demonstrations by famous chefs, talks, 'food cruises' round the harbour, and fringe events, including street theatre and children's entertainment. There's also eco-friendly fashion, skincare and homewares and, from 2008, a space for organic gardening demonstrations and advice, plus food trails and competitions. www.soilassociation.org/festival
STAY & EAT: on-site cafés and restaurants make for a wide choice of eating opportunities; the harbourside Bordeaux Quay, a restaurant, brasserie, bar, deli, bakery and cookery school, is worth singling out. There's also a member of the award-winning Hotel du Vin chain in Bristol. www.bordeaux-quay.co.uk;
www.hotelduvin.com

ALNWICK FOOD FESTIVAL

This pretty medieval market town has been hailed as the gastronomic capital of Northumberland. It is renowned as the location for the first Harry Potter film, and has hosted a weekend food festival every September since 2005, each bigger than the last and all focusing on local produce. Alnwick Beer Festival runs in parallel with the event, offering tastings of 30 real ales from 15 local breweries. The event also includes a Children's Food Festival. www.alnwickfoodfestival.co.uk
STAY & EAT: Alnwick has been described as a growing 'gastrohub' by virture of its food festival, farmers' markets and restaurants; the latter include The Treehouse in Alnwick Garden.
  Alnwick is about 60 km (40 miles) north of Newcastle, home to a Malmaison hotel with a brasserie offering a 'Homegrown & Local' menu featuring Holy Island oysters, farm honey and more Tyneside and Northumbria produce. www.alnwickgarden.com;
www.malmaison-newcastle.com

KINSALE GOURMET FESTIVAL

More fine food and drink – much of it local – is on the agenda at this festival in a medieval fishing port in south-east Ireland in October, with cookery demonstrations, wine tastings (including Fairtrade products), a champagne bar, cheeses and chocolates galore, and children's events, including a Mad Hatter's tea party. The highlight of the event, which has been running for more than 30 years, is a tour of the kitchens of the eleven restaurants belonging to Kinsale's Good Food Circle, which present their standout dishes. Special receptions and dinners can be attended too.
  Kinsale, south-east of Cork, has been dubbed 'the gourmet capital of Ireland' and is home to the International Wine Museum. www.kinsalerestaurants.com
STAY & EAT: The Blue Haven is a boutique-style hotel in Kinsale, with a restaurant, Blu, serving modern Irish fare with a global twist on a decked terrace in fine weather, a fish bistro and a café.
www.bluehavenkinsale.com

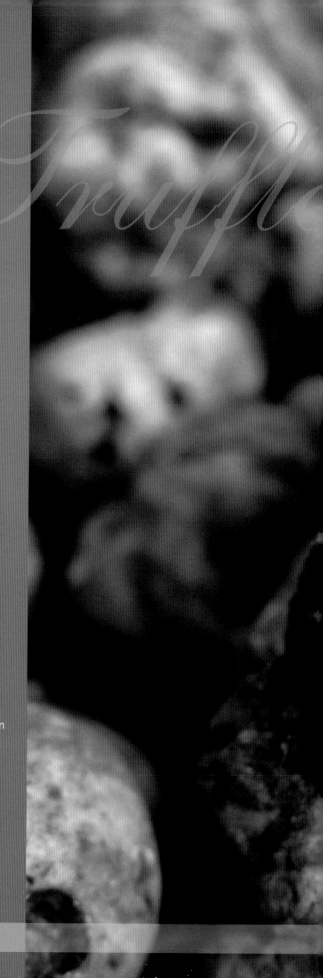

Italian Truffle Trail

With the truffle harvest spread from September until December, Autumn is the favourite season for aficionados of the fragrant fungus and of Italian cuisine in general.

FIERA NAZIONALE DEL TARTUFO BIANCO D'ALBA

October is the height of the white truffle season, with the highest prices and the fiercest competition among both hunters and buyers. Alba, in Piedmont, is Italy's truffle capital and main market as well as home to the Associazione Nazionale 'Città del Tartufo', representing nearly 20 truffle-producing towns in central Italy. Crowds of thousands converge on the town to sample local food and wine – including roast pork, salami, polenta, almond and chocolate cake, apricot cake, Gianduja chocolate, hazelnuts, and Moscato d'Alba wine.

There are further truffle fairs at Montiglio Monferrato, Moncalvo Monferrato and Ovada. www.fieradeltartufo.org; www.montigliom.at.it

STAY & EAT: the Ristorante Conti Roero is a striking brick-vaulted venue in Monticello d'Alba's 11th-century castle, 10 km (6 miles) from Alba. Cascina Baràc is a stunning *agriturismo* in Alba, with a restaurant terrace where you can enjoy Piedmont cuisine. www.contiroero.it; www.barac.it

SAN MINIATO SAGRA DEL TARTUFO BIANCO

The beautiful area around San Miniato in Tuscany produces around a quarter of Italy's white truffles, a fact celebrated by the quaint medieval town in its annual fair on the second, third and fourth weekends of November. As well as stalls and tastings with fresh truffles, there are open-air plays, marching bands, special menus in restaurants, and a local market.

Other white truffle fairs in the area take place in Balconevisi, usually on the third weekend in October, when the Sagra del Tartufo e del Fungo offers up olive oil, wine, walnuts, chestnuts, grapes and porcini; and in Volterra, a town best known for its Etruscan art, on the last weekend of October and first weekend of November. www.san-miniato.com

STAY & EAT: just south of San Miniato at Certaldo, the Castello del Nero in Chianti country is a restored 12th-century castle turned boutique hotel, with a spa and a restaurant, La Torre, serving fabulous Tuscan food and wine. www.castello-del-nero.com

Gourmet drive

SAN MINIATO
- Your starting point.

LIVORNO
- This port city is worth a stop-off for its Venice district, with canals, bridges and alleys, and for its *caciucco alla Livorne*, a fiery fish stew.

PISA
- Best known for its Leaning Tower, Pisa has plenty of eateries serving traditional Tuscan fare, including the local *baccalà alla Pisana* (dried cod).

LUCCA
- This laid-back and relatively untouristy town with its picturesque towers offers some of Tuscany's finest food, including its own *tortelli Lucchese*, a rich pasta stuffed with meat and then topped by a meaty *ragù*.

PRATO
- Tuscany's second largest city is a focal point of the Slow Food movement; its specialities include *sedani ripieni alla Pratese* – celery stuffed with mince, mortadella and nutmeg – and *cantuccini* biscuits.

FLORENCE
- The region's capital is a gourmet hotspot with numerous wonderful restaurants, many serving the Tuscan signature dish of *bistecca alla fiorentina*, a thick steak from local Chianina cattle.

Galway Oyster Fest

September in south-western Ireland is a treat for seafood and stout lovers, with oysters and Guinness galore.

The four-day Galway International Oyster Festival in western Ireland in late September – described by *The Sunday Times* as one of the twelve greatest shows on Earth – has been attracting seafood lovers from all over Ireland, Britain and the rest of the world for more than half a century. On offer are oysters, seafood chowder, smoked salmon, Guinness and wine tastings. In addition, there is the World Oyster Opening championship, live music – with the focus on traditional Irish song and dance – best-dressed competitions, a Mardi Gras party with jazz, a street parade with marching bands and vintage cars, and a black-tie ball. Some are free public events, others require tickets, with a proportion of the proceeds going to charity.

Earlier in the same month Clarenbridge, a few kilometres south of Galway, hosts its own three-day Oyster Festival, which has been held since 1954. As well as world-famous oysters, the Festival boasts a traditional market, talks and demonstrations, an art and photographic exhibition, the Black and White Ball, and the Sunday Jamboree, offering music and dancing, along with generous helpings of oysters, chowder and other seafood, and, inevitably, plenty of Guinness.

STAY & EAT

the g has cutting-edge interiors by hat designer Philip Treacy, inspired by the wild Galway coastline. Its restaurant, Riva at the g, serves modern Italian fare and global favourites amidst jewel-box décor. The spa has a rooftop bamboo garden. www.theghotel.ie/g/

Explore: *a Burren drive*

The Burren to the south of Galway is a landscape of carboniferous limestone plateaux crisscrossed by grykes (cracks) and famous for its rare flowers, Celtic crosses, villages abandoned during the Famine and abundance of megalithic ruins.

GALWAY
- Your starting and finishing point.

CORCOMROE ABBEY
- In the north of the Burren, this splendid ruined Cistercian monastery dating from the 12th century boasts detailed, and unique, botanical carvings.

AILLWEE CAVES
- These 2-million-year-old caves lead to the heart of the Burren's underground with its vast caves and rivers. Guided tours reveal animal remains, waterfalls and impressive cave formations.

CORKSCREW HILL
- On a clear day, the viewing point high on this hill offers a wonderful vista of Galway Bay.

KILFENORA
- This village at the Burren's southern tip is home to a partly ruined 12th-century cathedral, as well as the Burren Display Centre showcasing the region's plantlife and wildlife.

LEAMANEAGH CASTLE
- This magnificent ruin comprises a fortified 16th-century manor built onto a late-15th-century tower.

Galway | Corcomroe Abbey | Aillwee Caves | Corkscrew Hill | Kilfenora | Leamaneagh Castle

Autumn Horse Events

Autumn brings some of the year's best horse racing together with some of the sport's biggest social occasions.

ST LEGER FESTIVAL AND THE TOTE HANDICAP

First run in 1776, the St Leger Stakes is a flat race for three-year-old thoroughbred colts and fillies. It is the world's oldest Classic race, and the only one staged by a racecourse in the north of England – Doncaster's Town Moor, which has been completely redeveloped in the past few years. During the four-day festival, held in mid-September, marquees are erected by the winning post, the lawned former paddock area and by the centre of the course, offering champagne and food.

Also staged at the racecourse is the Tote November Handicap, held to celebrate the last day of the British Flat season and featuring end-of-season awards and a party, with presentations to the champion trainer, owner, jockey and apprentice. First run at Manchester Racecourse in 1876, it transferred to Doncaster in 1964. www.doncaster-racecourse.co.uk

STAY & EAT: The Crown Hotel at Bawtry, 14 km (9 miles) from Doncaster, has chic contemporary bedrooms and suites and a restaurant offering a 'Yorkshire Tapas' menu of locally sourced food. www.crownhotel-bawtry.com

THE OPEN CHELTENHAM

Britain's most important meeting of the first half of the Jump season offers three days of top-class racing in mid-November. It begins with the immensely popular Countryside Raceday (Friday), featuring falconry displays and hound parades, as well as the season's first cross-country steeplechase. The next day sees the prestigious Paddy Power Gold Cup, and on Sunday there's the fiercely fought Greatwood Handicap Hurdle. www.cheltenham.co.uk

STAY: the Alias Kandinsky Hotel in central Cheltenham. www.aliashotels.com/kandinsky

HENNESSY WINTER FESTIVAL

Newbury Racecourse's three-day festival draws thousands of race fans to Berkshire in late November for the flagship National Hunt race, the prestigious handicap Hennessy Cognac Gold Cup for five-year-olds and above, featuring 21 fences. Guests can choose from the Racegoers Restaurant and the elegant Hennessy Restaurant with its panoramic views. www.newbury-racecourse.co.uk

STAY & EAT: The Vineyard has rooms named after wines, a spa and a Michelin-starred restaurant. www.the-vineyard.co.uk

STAN JAMES CHRISTMAS FESTIVAL

The idyllic Kempton Park racecourse between Sunbury-on-Thames and Hampton Court attracts the best Jump racers for its two-day festival offering a huge £650,000 in prize money. The first day, Boxing Day, hosts the now legendary King George VI Steeplechase, which celebrated the new king's ascent to the throne in 1937. On 27 December, the Desert Orchid Chase commemorates the great horse who raced here. www.kempton.co.uk

STAY & EAT: for hotels and restaurants in nearby Richmond, see pp.18 and 71.

"Four things greater than all things are, Women and Horses and Power and War."

Rudyard Kipling

Prix de l'Arc de Triomphe

The first Sunday in October sees the winners of many of the top-class races from around Europe compete in one of the French racing season's four Classic events.

Dating back to 1920, the Prix de l'Arc de Triomphe was a complement to the Grand Prix de Paris. This race began in 1863 and was open to three-year-olds from around the globe; some 30 years later it was amended to attract older horses, and became extremely successful with foreign owners. The 'Arc' was named in tribute to the French soldiers who had served their country in the First World War. In 2008 it became the most richly rewarded turf race in the world when its purse doubled to 4 million euros. It now attracts an audience of more than 60,000 people.

An inter-generational flat race without handicapping for thoroughbreds, L'Arc is run on the 2.4-km (1.5-mile) turf track at Longchamp racecourse beside the Bois de Boulogne in western Paris. Comprising an uphill and downhill slope with a notoriously testing rise out of the final bend, the course requires both speed and stamina.

A day at the races here remains as traditional and glamorous as the English Derby, enhanced by the presence of the iconic 1856 windmill, which gives its name to the Prix du Moulin.

STAY & EAT
Le Meurice is a classic choice near the Louvre, amidst Paris's most chic boutiques, with Philippe Starck designed reception areas, a new spa and two restaurants. www.lemeurice.com

For more Paris hotels and restaurants, see pp.96 and 123.

"A canter is a cure for every evil."

Benjamin Disraeli

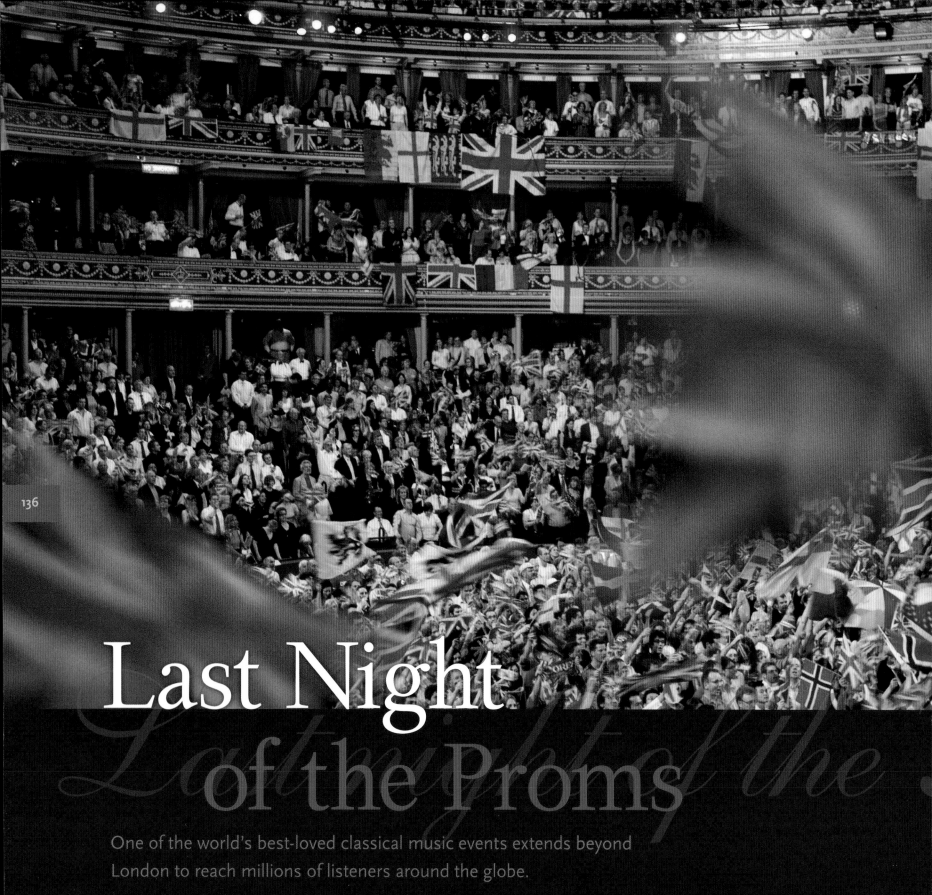

Last Night
of the Proms

One of the world's best-loved classical music events extends beyond
London to reach millions of listeners around the globe.

Proms

The largest classical music festival on Earth, comprising more than 80 concerts, the eight-week BBC Proms, running from July to September, was founded in 1895. The name derives from 'promenade concerts' – the audience used to be able to stroll around some parts of the hall during the concert, and today holders of the least expensive tickets stand in the arena and gallery in front of the orchestra.

The Proms culminates in the Last Night party, usually on the second Saturday in September, which brings together the various themes of the Prom season. It has a lighthearted feel, beginning with popular classics and moving on to patriotic British works – Elgar's *Pomp and Circumstance March No. 1 (Land of Hope and Glory)*, Sir Henry Wood's *Fantasia on British Sea Songs*, which ends with Thomas Arne's *Rule Britannia*, Hubert Parry's *Jerusalem* and then the National Anthem. Some of the audience wear patriotic T-shirts, others dinner jackets. Union Jacks are waved during *Rule Britannia*.

Seats for the final night sell out quickly; to get a ticket one must also attend several other Proms in the season. Prom tickets are no more expensive for the Last Night than for other concerts, but many prommers queue overnight and all day to get a good space. To accommodate some of the many people who can't get a ticket, a Proms in the Park concert is held in Hyde Park opposite the Royal Albert Hall, the Proms' main venue. A live big-screen links up with the hall for the finale and people usually get into the spirit outside too.

> "Music should strike fire from the heart of man, and bring tears from the eyes of woman."
>
> Ludvig Van Beethoven

137

AUTUMN

STAY & EAT

Brown's Hotel in Mayfair is a bastion of classic British style, with a genteel wood-panelled tea-room. There's also a luxurious spa. Closer to the Royal Albert Hall, the Mandarin Oriental Hyde Park has opulent rooms, an award-winning spa and two restaurants.

Beside Hyde Park, Nobu London is fêted for its 'new-style' Japanese cuisine, which has earned it a Michelin star. Around the corner on Upper Brook Street, Le Gavroche is famous for its French cuisine by Michel Roux, holder of two Michelin stars. www.brownshotel.com; www.mandarinoriental.com/london; www.noburestaurants.com; www.le-gavroche.co.uk

Braemar Gathering

The heather-clad hills of Braemar, west of Aberdeen, are host to this world-famous event showcasing traditional Scottish sports and games.

Braemar, in the Cairngorms National Park, has hosted gatherings of one kind or another for 900 years, since the time of King Malcolm Canmore. The current Gathering, which takes place on the first Saturday in September, dates back to 1832, making it one of Scotland's oldest Highland gatherings, as well as one of its largest. Substantial crowds come to watch athletes from around the world compete in 'heavy' and 'track' events, including a tug-of-war by teams from the armed forces, a Services relay race, caber-tossing, stone-putting, sprinting, hammer-throwing, a hill race and a long leap. There's also Highland dancing, massed pipe bands and a children's sack race.

Queen Victoria was very fond of the Gathering, first attending it in 1848, and today The Queen still comes to Braemar regularly and is hailed as the event's chieftain. Seats (grandstand, uncovered and ringside) sell out long in advance, but it is also possible to view events from the hills and terraces within the grounds.

Drive: *to Braemar*

Starting at Edinburgh, take a scenic route all the way to Braemar.

BLAIRGOWRIE

○ North of Edinburgh, via the Forth Bridge and Perth, lies this red-stone town beside the River Ericht, at the point where it emerges from the breathtaking Strathmore gorges. Nearby Rosemount Golf Course is considered one of the finest inland courses in Scotland, while the Loch of Lowes between Blairgowrie and Dunkeld is a Scottish Wildlife Trust reserve with otters and rare ospreys.

SPITTAL OF GLENSHEE

○ Due north of Blairgowrie is Scotland's largest skiing area, with superb scenery. The town of Glenshee itself has a wide choice of ski-hire shops and ski schools.

BALLATER

○ East of Braemar, picturesque Ballater is a former spa resort with many Victorian buildings – its centre is a conservation area. It's also a base for hiking in the area, which has many munros. Balmoral Castle, the Royal Family's holiday home, is just to the west, and many of the town's shops have Royal Warrants. From here it is a stunning drive to Braemar.

STAY & EAT

Braemar's Invercauld Castle is an exclusive venue for parties of 6 to 24 people. The plush rooms include The Prince's Suite used by Queen Victoria. The kitchen provides meals to order, and there's grouse and partridge shooting, deer-stalking and salmon fishing on the estate.
www.invercauldcastle.com

For restaurant recommendations in Edinburgh, see pp.109 and 168.

"Land of brown
heath and
shaggy wood,
Land of the
mountain
and the flood,
Land of my sires!
What mortal hand
Can e'er untie…"

Sir Walter Scott

Munich Oktoberfest

The world's biggest beer and folk festival brings an astonishing six million visitors to the Bavarian city every year.

The Oktoberfest first took place over six days in mid-October 1810, to celebrate the Crown Prince Ludwig's marriage to Princess Therese von Sachsen-Hildburghausen. Locals have nicknamed the festival 'die Wiesn' because of its setting, the open space of Theresienwiese to the south of the centre, where Therese and Ludwig wed.

The current festival now lasts just over two weeks, ending on the first weekend in October. The event opens on a Saturday with a midday ceremony in the Schottenhamel tent, when the city's Lord Mayor taps the first keg of beer and shares its contents around; many people arrive at 9am to get good seats. The highlight is the costume and riflemen's parade the following day. There's also a parade of landlords and breweries with decorated carriages and floats and horse-drawn drays, a *Böllerschießen* (handheld canon salute) in front of the Bavaria statue, and rollercoasters, fairground rides and sideshows. Each Tuesday is a Family Day with discounts on entrance and rides.

MUNICH HIGHLIGHTS

Art-lovers head for the Kunstareal ('art district'), home to the Alte Pinakothek, Neue Pinakothek and Pinakothek der Moderne galleries, and to the Lenbachhaus Kunstbau with its important collection of European pieces, including several Kandinskys. The Deutsches Museum, set on an island in the Isar, is one of the world's biggest – and most longstanding – science museums. Meanwhile, shoppers will find designer labels aplenty on the Maximilianstrasse.

Munich is also surrounded by a variety of scenic golf courses and wonderful hiking spots. There are boat trips and Alp views on the stunning Starnberger See. The fairytale-like Neuschwanstein, once home to Ludwig II, is one of the world's most iconic castles (it inspired the designs for Cinderella's and Sleeping Beauty's castles in Disneyland).

STAY & EAT

It's essential to book accommodation as far in advance as possible for this popular event; packages including a hotel and festival entry are available. The Charles Hotel, part of the chic Rocco Forte collection, offers faultlessly tasteful rooms and suites, a spa with a swimming pool, and an elegant Italian restaurant with views over the garden from its terrace. www.charleshotel.de

London to Brighton
Veteran Car Run

hton

The longest-running motoring event in the world gives spectators the chance to see characterful veteran cars making a rare foray onto the streets.

R un by the Royal Automobile Club, this high-spirited event on the first Sunday of November brings more than 500 owners of pre-1905 cars from all over the world to make the 96-km (60-mile) run from London's Hyde Park to the Brighton seafront. Many cars are shipped specially for the event from as far afield as the States and New Zealand.

The rally came into being in 1896, in the form of an Emancipation Run celebrating the Locomotives on the Highway Act, which raised the speed limit for 'light locomotives' from 4 mph to 14 mph and abolished the need for these vehicles to be preceded by a person on foot waving a red flag. The next Run, in 1927, re-enacted the first; the event was henceforth annual, with the exception of the Second World War years. Sometimes celebrities, including Royals, take part.

On the Friday preceding the rally, auction house Bonhams stages an auction of veteran cars that are eligible to join in the event, as well as automobilia, while on the eve of the rally a concourse in Regent Street showcases more than 100 of the cars, and some of the vehicles make demonstration runs along

Conduit Street and around Berkeley Square. Spectating is free all along the route: Norbury, Croydon, Purley, Redhill, Horley, Gatwick, Crawley, Cuckfield, Burgess Hill and then towns and villages _en route_ to Brighton. More than a million spectators line this route, so it is essential to arrive early to get a good view. Cars begin leaving Hyde Park Corner in twos at sunrise (just before 7am) and travel at about 32 km/h (20 mph), with the first vehicles arriving at Brighton's seafront Marine Parade at 10am and the last puttering in at around 4.30pm.

STAY & EAT

Drakes Hotel on the seafront is a boutique townhouse with restrained contemporary décor and a restaurant, The Gingerman, strong on local seafood.

Due South, situated on the promenade between the two piers, was named Britain's Best Seaside Restaurant by the _Observer Food Monthly_.

Terre à Terre has also won plaudits for its inventive vegetarian food. www.drakesofbrighton.com; www.duesouth.co.uk; www.terreaterre.co.uk

"A person with half volition goes backwards and forwards, but makes no progress on even the smoothest of roads."

Thomas Carlyle

Le Sap Cider Festival

Normandy is the setting for a lively festival celebrating the bounty of the apple harvest in a region that is famous for its fine cider, Calvados, pommeau and apple juice.

STAY & EAT

About 40 km (25 miles) from Le Sap, towards Argentan, Le Pavillon du Gouffern is a former hunting lodge with rolling lawns, a tennis court, an outdoor pool, stylish rooms and excellent cuisine championing local ingredients. www.pavillondegouffern.com

The second weekend of November sees the picturesque town of Le Sap, a heritage site with half-timbered medieval houses, host its Fête du Cidre à l'Ancienne, showcasing the traditional cider made from the region's 300-plus apple varieties.

The event takes place over two days in the town's marketplace and in the Grand Jardin, winner of awards for green tourism. Visitors can watch juice being pressed in a mill powered by sturdy local Percheron horses, as well as demonstrations of local crafts, study 18th-century cider-making machinery, buy local produce and enjoy live music. There are food and drink stalls aplenty, and the site has its own restaurant serving local dishes.

Le Grand Jardin is also home to the permanent Ecomusée de la Pomme au Calvados, on an old cider-and-Calvados farm site, displaying old machinery and tools, and offering tastings. There's also a conservation orchard with a trail through the apple trees that produce cider boasting the *Origine Contrôlée Pays d'Auge* mark of quality.

THE CALVADOS CIDER ROUTE

North-west of Le Sap, you'll find this signposted circular tourist route through the Calvados countryside dotted with orchards, stud farms, châteaux, old manor houses and half-timbered dwellings. The signpost 'Cru de Cambremer' means that a small-scale local producer (there are almost 20 on the 50-km/ 30-mile route, marked on the map on the website) offers cellar tours and tastings. www.calvados-tourisme.com

Lewes Fireworks

Lewes, the picturesque county town of East Sussex, is famed for its Bonfire Night celebrations attracting up to 80,000 revellers.

Lewes has seven bonfire societies, six of which participate in the event. Members embark on torchlit processions through the town, with each society taking its own particular route and boasting its own costume, be it Tudor or Native American. Huge effigies are carried, including those of Guy Fawkes and Pope Paul V (who was pontiff when the martyrs were burned), and one society even displays on pikes the heads of 'Enemies of Bonfire', which might be local officials or national figures. The effigies are then thrown onto bonfires at five different locations around town, each of which is accompanied by a stunning firework display.

OTHER DISPLAYS

Other noteworthy Bonfire Night celebrations around the country include: Weymouth in Dorset, featuring a bonfire on the beach, a funfair and fireworks over the bay; Winchester in Hampshire, which stages a torchlit procession through its medieval centre; and Leeds Castle in Kent, which hosts pyrotechnic spectaculars with lights and music. In London, outstanding firework displays take place in Battersea Park and at Alexandra Palace, the latter including ice-skating. www.weymouth.gov.uk; www.hants.gov.uk; www.leeds-castle.com; www.wandsworth.gov.uk; www.alexandrapalace.com

Though Guy Fawkes Night celebrations are held around the country on or around the 5th November, the best-known event takes place in the town of Lewes in East Sussex. Here the townspeople, together with visitors from around the southeast and further afield, commemorate not only the discovery of the Gunpowder Plot in 1605 but also the burning at the stake of 17 Protestant martyrs in the 16th century, by carrying 17 burning crosses through the streets and laying a wreath at the town's war memorial.

STAY & EAT

Pelham House in Lewes itself is a 16th-century townhouse with stylish contemporary rooms and a restaurant serving 'classic modern' dishes against a backdrop of the Sussex Downs.

Newick Park, north of Lewes, is a country house with parkland views from its smart bedrooms, and its restaurant uses fruit and vegetables from the hotel's own walled garden and game from its estate.

The Real Eating Company in Lewes offers modern English food and seasonal ingredients. www.pelhamhouse.com; www.newickpark.co.uk; www.real-eating.co.uk

As the old year wanes, fight off the winter blues. Enjoy a winter walk through a frosty landscape, ski over pristine snow, or drive along deserted roads that meander over mist-shrouded hills. Visit a country hotel and drink claret in front of a blazing fire. At this time of year, city lights illuminate the early twilight, offering a cornucopia of festive shops, foods, parties and entertainments. Carnival celebrations signal that the long winter hibernation is ending; streets bright with multi-coloured costumes are a reminder that spring is not far away.

Winter

487 YGS

"Winter, a lingering
season, is a time
to gather golden
moments, embark
upon a sentimental
journey, and enjoy
every idle hour…"

John Boswell

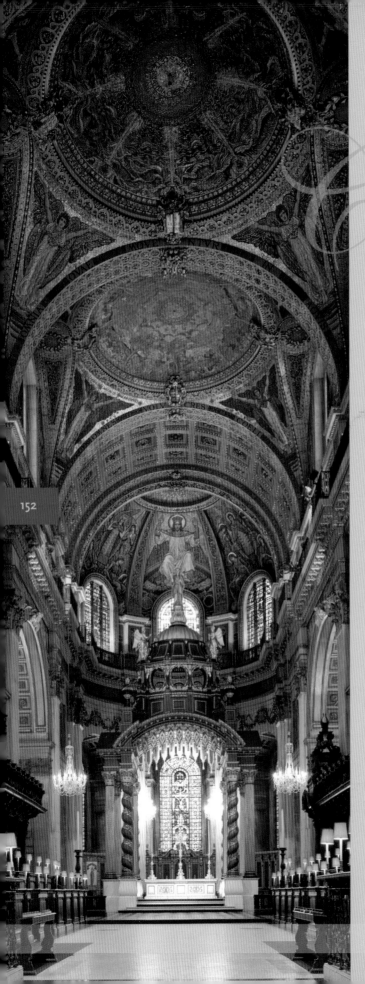

Christmas Carols

Get into the Christmas spirit with a carol service in an English cathedral. Enjoy the magnificent choirs, traditional readings and festive favourites in beautiful, historic surroundings.

Canterbury Cathedral

This imposing cathedral is the seat of the Archbishop of Canterbury and is perhaps most famous as the place where Archbishop Thomas Becket was murdered in 1170.
www.canterbury-cathedral.org
STAY: Hotel Relish in Folkstone.
www.hotelrelish.co.uk

Durham Cathedral

Durham Cathedral forms part of a World Heritage Site with Durham Castle. This impressive Norman cathedral sits in grandeur upon a hill overlooking the city. www.durhamcathedral.co.uk
STAY: Seaham Hall.
www.seaham-hall.com

Wells Cathedral

Don't miss the breathtaking west façade, containing over 300 original medieval statues, the 14th-century stained-glass, and the octagonal Chapter with its beautiful fan vaulting. www.wellscathedral.org.uk
STAY: Millers at Glencote House.
www.glencotehouse.co.uk

Westminster Abbey, London

This wonderful building is known as the House of Kings, where monarchs have been crowned and buried since 1066. Visit the South Transept for Poets' Corner.
www.westminster-abbey.org
STAY: The Savoy.
www.fairmont.com/savoy

Winchester Cathedral

Founded in 1079, this stunning building is famous for its chantry chapels, within which many bishops are buried.
www.winchestercathedral.org.uk
STAY: The Winchester Hotel.
www.pedersenhotels.com

York Minster

This Gothic masterpiece contains vibrant stained-glass windows and a beautiful Chapter House. Climb to the top of the central tower for a panoramic view over York's winding streets.
www.yorkminster.org
STAY: Four High Petergate.
www.fourhighpetergate.co.uk

carols

OTHER DESTINATIONS

Bristol Cathedral
www.bristol-cathedral.co.uk
STAY: Hotel du Vin Bristol.
www.hotelduvin.com

Chester Cathedral
www.chestercathedral.com
STAY: The Chester Green Bough Hotel.
www.chestergreenbough.com

Ely Cathedral
www.elycathedral.org
STAY: The Anchor Inn, Sutton Gault.
www.anchor-inn-restaurant.co.uk

Exeter Cathedral
www.exeter-cathedral.org.uk
STAY: Alias Hotel Barcelona.
www.aliashotels.com/barcelona

King's College, Cambridge
www.kings.cam.ac.uk/chapel
STAY: Hotel du Vin Cambridge.
www.hotelduvin.com

St Paul's Cathedral, London
www.stpauls.co.uk
STAY: Covent Garden Hotel.
www.firmdale.com

> "I will honour Christmas in my heart, and try to keep it all the year."
>
> Charles Dickens

Check cathedral websites from the end of September to find out what is planned. Look out for cathedrals with concerts featuring their own choirs as they will have developed a sound that complements the building's acoustics.

There may be free recitals, but some services require advance tickets – book early as the famous cathedral services are often in demand. Be sure to arrive early at free concerts to get a good seat.

Ice Skating

Frosty air, roasting chestnuts, skates skimming nimbly across the ice... Whatever your skating prowess, there are plenty of unusual places to triumph or topple.

LONDON

Somerset House

This gracious 18th-century riverside palace is one of the most beautiful settings in London, especially when it is illuminated at night. Be ready 15 minutes in advance to make the most of your time on the ice.

Natural History Museum

The Romanesque towers of this magnificent Victorian landmark dominate the skyline of South Kensington. It is a superb winter ice location, but it can get crowded. Hollywood A-listers have been spotted here, gliding across the ice.

Hampton Court Palace

One of the finest palaces in Europe, this Tudor masterpiece built for Cardinal Wolsey on the banks of the Thames is a dramatic backdrop, and the scene is romantically reminiscent of medieval frost fairs.

Tower of London

Founded over a millennium ago, the Tower of London was the last sight on earth for many Tudor luminaries and traitors. Enjoy a pleasurable frisson as you skate around this good-sized rink within the moat.

Kew Gardens

This imposing 1,000-square-metre rink is located in front of the Temperate House, the world's largest surviving Victorian glass structure, built between 1859 and 1862.

Greenwich Old Royal Naval College

This spectacular historic venue, originally a naval hospital overlooking the River Thames, dates back to the early 18th century, and was conceived by Sir Christopher Wren. Visit nearby Charlton House, a beautifully preserved Jacobean mansion, once your skating is done.

ELSEWHERE

East Princes Street Gardens, Edinburgh

Children will love Edinburgh's impressive Winter Wonderland.

Eden Project, Cornwall

A truly unique location; enjoy exploring the biospheres after you have finished skating.

Millennium Square, Leeds

A family-friendly rink known as the 'Ice Cube', in the heart of the city.

Piccadilly, Manchester

Skate in the centre of this buzzing city. Beginners can take a six-week 'learn to skate' course.

Place de l'Hôtel de Ville, Paris

The skating is free, but you have to hire a pair of skates for a few euros.

Warwick Castle

An ice trail allows visitors to skate through the castle grounds.

"Skating is a chilly pleasure, and therefore, no sin."

Heinrich Heine

European
Christmas Markets

Escape the pre-Christmas panic and imbibe the seasonal atmosphere with a leisurely road trip around some magical festive markets.

Dating to the Middle Ages, these enchanting markets are atmospheric and traditional. Shoppers are serenaded by carol singers, and tempted by delicious nibbles and the odd glass of something mulled – a delightful alternative to the busy high street. The markets focus on local arts and crafts and handmade Christmas decorations, so get your big presents in hand well before you leave.

ANTWERP (Dec)
The Cathedral Of Our Lady is the tallest Gothic church in Europe, and the Grote Markt to its west hosts the annual Christmas market. Antwerp is a key player in the world diamond trade – head for the Diamant tram station where the diamond district boasts some 2,500 diamond companies and shops.
STAY: Hotel Julien, elegant and contemporary. www.hotel-julien.com

COPENHAGEN (Nov–Dec)
The beautiful Tivoli Gardens have a fairytale atmosphere, with hundreds of Christmas trees and thousands of lights. There's skating on the lake and lashings of glögg – a Danish mulled wine mixed with liquor and spices.
STAY: the stylish Front Hotel. www.front.dk

BRUSSELS (Nov–Dec)
Over 200 stalls around the Bourse (stock exchange), Marché aux Poissons (fish market) and Place Sainte-Catherine offer indulgences from all over Europe. There is also a splendid ice rink at the Marché aux Poissons.
STAY: Hôtel Métropole. www.metropolehotel.com

STRASBOURG (Nov–Dec)
Strasbourg Cathedral, with its Gothic towers and famous astronomical clock, is a breathtaking setting for this ancient market. Well worth a visit is La Petite France, an area of picturesque buildings with Christmas shops and a gingerbread bakery.
STAY: Hotel Regent Petite France. www.regent-petite-france.com

COLOGNE (Nov–Dec)
The Cathedral Christmas Market dominates the square in front of the twin spires of Cologne's famous Gothic cathedral, and is clustered around a huge Christmas tree. Further south, the market on the Alter Markt, in front of the town hall, offers some truly festive treats for children, from numerous toy stands to a merry-go-round.
STAY: Excelsior Hotel Ernst, near the cathedral. www.excelsiorhotelernst.de

NUREMBERG (Nov–Dec)
This famous market dates back to 1628, offering some 200 stalls in the cobbled square beneath the Frauenkirche. Be sure to try spicy Nürnberg bratwurst and soft, gingerbread-like Lebkuchen.
STAY: the art deco Meridien Grand Hotel. www.grand-hotel.de

BADEN-BADEN (Nov–Dec)

The Christkindelsmarkt nestles under the glamorous Kurhaus, the focal point of this famous spa town. Choirs, orchestras and bands all help to make this market a delight.
STAY: Hotel Belle Epoque, a stunning neo-renaissance villa surrounded by parkland.
www.hotel-belle-epoque.de

DRESDEN (Nov–Dec)

The quaint Striezelmark is the oldest of Germany's markets, named after Striezel (Dresden's famous fruit loaf, nowadays known as Stollen). The Stollen Festival, held on the Saturday before the second Sunday in Advent, is a popular attraction.
STAY: Hotel Bülow Residenz with its Michelin-starred restaurant The Caroussel.
www.buelow-residenz.de

BERN (Dec)

Münsterplatz is the largest of the markets, found amid the Old Town houses. Don't miss the nearby Waisenhausplatz and Stöbern markets.
STAY: Bellevue Palace Hotel.
www.bellevue-palace.ch

St Nicholas Fayre Market, York

The Gothic spires, cobbled streets and timbered medieval houses of York are a tranquil antidote to frenzied, commercialised high streets. Soak up York's wintry charm while exploring the Christmas Markets, including the ever-popular St Nicholas Fayre.

The annual St Nicholas Fayre Market, at the end of November, offers a selection of stalls across the city, including Parliament Street, St Sampson's Square, Kings Square, Coppergate and the Guildhall. A medieval market is also re-created at Barley Hall, a historic townhouse in the heart of the city.

This seasonal market is a foodie's mecca, offering local farm produce such as venison and boar. Wander among the stalls displaying arts and crafts, and don't forget to sample some mulled wine, hot chocolate and roasted chestnuts.

YORK
○ The start and end point.

MALTON
○ Don't miss nearby Castle Howard, one of the most impressive stately homes in the country. The grounds cover nearly 1,000 acres – perfect for a winter walk.

PICKERING
○ This historic market town is the southern terminus of the North Yorkshire Moors Railway, and is the official gateway to the North York Moors National Park.

Explore: *the Dales*

Drive across the frost-tinged dales and enjoy panoramas of snowy, smoke-wreathed villages.

STAY
Four High Petergate is a gorgeous Georgian townhouse; Marmadukes Hotel is a former Victorian gentlemen's residence. Both are a short stroll from the Minster. www.fourhighpetergate.co.uk; www.marmadukeshotels.co.uk

EAT
Bettys Café Tea Rooms for afternoon tea; for dinner, try Baker's Bistro Moderne. www.bettys.co.uk; www.jbakers.co.uk

DRIVE & DINE
The Durham Ox in Crayke. www.thedurhamox.com
The Star Inn near Helmsley. www.thestaratharome.co.uk
The Yorke Arms near Harrogate. www.yorke-arms.co.uk

VISIT
The Yorkshire Sculpture Park in West Bretton features modern and contemporary sculpture set in the 500-acre grounds of the Bretton estate. www.ysp.co.uk

GOATHLAND
○ This picture-postcard Yorkshire village was the location for the television series *Heartbeat*.

GROSMONT
○ This is the northern terminus of the North Yorkshire Moors Railway, attracting many steam locomotive enthusiasts.

DANBY
○ Look out for the Scotch Blackface sheep on the village green.

HELMSLEY
○ Visit the medieval ruins of Helmsley Castle.

Winter Walks

A winter stroll through one of London's Royal Parks offers some respite from the city in the winter and a great day out for visitors.

160

BUSHY PARK

At just over 1,000 acres, Bushy Park is the second largest of the Royal Parks. It was once a hunting ground for Henry VIII and his daughter Elizabeth, and you may still spot a roaming red or fallow deer – there are approximately 320 in the park. The mile-long Chestnut Avenue features the magnificent Arethusa 'Diana' Fountain.

DETAILS: open to pedestrians 24 hours, except September and November (8am–10.30pm). Entrances on Hampton Court Road (A308) and Sandy Lane (B358).
DON'T MISS: Hampton Court Palace. www.hrp.org.uk/hamptoncourtpalace

KENSINGTON GARDENS

Kensington Gardens were once part of Hyde Park but, in 1689, William III bought this tranquil spot and commissioned Sir Christopher Wren to design Kensington Palace. Queen Anne extended the land further and created the Orangery in 1704; today the gardens cover 275 acres.

The Italian Gardens and the Albert Memorial were both commissioned by Queen Victoria. Don't miss the famous statue of Peter Pan near the Longwater.

DETAILS: open all year, 6am to dusk. Parking is limited. Nearest Underground stations: Lancaster Gate, Queensway and High Street Kensington.
DON'T MISS: Serpentine Gallery.
www.serpentinegallery.org

ROYAL BOTANIC GARDENS, KEW

Kew Gardens, a UNESCO World Heritage site, were originally the gardens of Kew Palace.George III pioneered a scheme to collect specimens of plants from all over the world, making Kew a famous centre of botanic research. Winter highlights include winter-flowering cherries, camellias and the impressive Alpine House.

DETAILS: Kew Gardens is well signposted. Parking is available near the Brentford Gate, reached via Ferry Lane off Kew Green. Opening times vary; check before visiting. www.kew.org
DON'T MISS: the 'Kew Explorer' will make sure you see everything the gardens have to offer.

RICHMOND PARK, SURREY

In 1625, Charles I moved to Richmond Palace to escape the plague. He created a hunting park, introducing red and fallow deer to the land. At 2,500 acres, Richmond Park is the largest of London's Royal Parks.

The park is famous for its varied birdlife and is a haven for numerous species, from kestrels to parakeets. Some 650 deer roam the park, amongst imposing stands of ancient oaks.

DETAILS: there are six visitor car parks; use the Broomfield Hill car park (entrance gates on A3 or A308). Open from 7am (summer) and 7.30am (winter); closes at dusk.
DON'T MISS: Pembroke Lodge, a Georgian mansion. www.pembroke-lodge.co.uk

European Skiing Destinations

Whether you are a serious skier or a committed shopper and party animal, you will find some of the world's great ski destinations within easy reach in Europe. Snowfall can be unpredictable and the length of the skiing season can last from early winter into late spring.

KLOSTERS, SWITZERLAND

Situated in the Rega Pass Area, Klosters offers over 320 km (200 miles) of perfect powder snow and excellent runs. Still a favourite with British royalty, it exudes quiet, romantic charm and an air of exclusivity. Try a leisurely 12-km (7-mile) run to the village of Küblis, followed by some off-piste shopping in the neighbouring town of Davos. There are over 100 stores, boutiques and art galleries in the streets around the Davos Platz. Don't miss the impressive 11-minute cable-car ride from Klosters to Madrisa; there are some fabulous hiking trails to explore from the top.
STAY: Chesa Grischuna, an elegant, historical town centre hotel. www.chesagrischuna.ch

ST MORITZ, SWITZERLAND

Still the quintessential destination for skiers and dedicated fashionistas, St Moritz offers 350 km (215 miles) of slopes, a wealth of snow-based activities and some serious shopping. The slopes range from beginner to intermediate; Celerina is the place for novices. Experts tend to head off-piste for excitement and exhilaration. Cross-country skiing is particularly good and, for serious thrill seekers, the Cresta Run is found here. In January and February, cricket, polo and horse racing take place on the frozen lake.
STAY: the glitzy Badrutt's Palace or the well located Hotel Kulm. www.badruttspalace.com; www.kulmhotel-stmoritz.ch

VERBIER, SWITZERLAND

Verbier is widely regarded as one of the more difficult arenas because of the challenging off-piste opportunities. The unmarked Stairway to Heaven and Hidden Valley runs are some of the best, but should only be attempted with a guide. Experts flock to the 3,000-m (9,840-ft) Mont Fort; Les Ruinettes and Les Attelas are easier going.
STAY: Hotel Nevai boasts a bar with a 4 metre-long fireplace and a restaurant with spectacular views. www.nevai.ch

ZERMATT, SWITZERLAND

Zermatt boasts one of the longest ski seasons in Europe, lasting until late April or early May. Dominated by the Matterhorn and surrounded by a ring of mountains, Zermatt lies just kilometres from the Italian border. Take the cable-car up Klein Matterhorn to the highest accessible viewing platform in Europe.

Skiing is divided into three areas: Sunnegga, Gonergrat and Klein Matterhorn. There is a sophisticated lift system of trams and gondolas – the mountains are too high for ski lifts. There are vast, scenic ski areas on offer, with long runs, some lasting more than 11 km (7 miles). Most of the terrain is suited to more advanced skiers.

Zermatt offers peaceful, car-free cobbled streets – horse-drawn sleighs are a common

sight. There are plenty of excellent restaurants and nightspots centred around the main Bahnhofstrasse.
STAY: The Omnia, set high on a rock, with a lobby at more than 1,600 metres (5,250 ft) above sea-level. www.the-omnia.com

ARLBERG SKI CIRCUS, AUSTRIA

This extensive area of interlinked resorts offers some of the best, and most exclusive, skiing in Europe.

ST ANTON: it has been claimed to be one of the best ski resorts in the world, with good snow virtually guaranteed from December to April. With a reputation for tough terrain more suited to advanced skiers, this popular destination is famous for its slopes as well as its après-ski.
STAY: the family run Raffl's St Antoner Hof. www.antonerhof.at

ST CHRISTOPH: this tiny resort is one of the highest in the Alps, at 1,800 metres (5,905 ft) above sea-level. Home of the prestigious Arlberg Ski Club, this resort offers unrivalled slopes and peaceful exclusivity.
STAY: the opulent Arlberg Hospiz Hotel offers extremely luxurious rooms. www.hospiz.com

ZÜRS: pristine slopes offer fantastic skiing. Numbers are restricted, allowing this resort to maintain its perfect condition and exclusive feel. Not suited to beginners.
STAY: the well-located Hotel Zürserhof. www.zuerserhof.at

LECH: famous for its 14th-century spire, this upmarket village offers good conditions and famous slopes, and is well-suited to non-skiers (think designer shopping).
STAY: Hotel Gasthof Post's award-winning restaurant boasts an impressive wine list. www.postlech.com

KITZBÜHEL, AUSTRIA

Kitzbühel, with over 170 km (105 miles) of slopes, caters well for all abilities. Experts head to the Hahnenkamm course where the World Cup men's downhill is held each year. The winding streets offer cosy bars and cafés, which can get busy at night, suiting those after boisterous après-ski. Kitzbühel's smooth, grassy slopes require relatively little snow for good skiing. Should it prove patchy, charter a guide for a Ski Safari from Pengelstein to the Jochberg/Pass Thurn area.
STAY: Relais & Châteaux Hotel Tennerhof, originally a farmhouse dating back to the 17th century. www.tennerhof.com

CORTINA, ITALY

This fashionable Italian resort in the Ampezzo Valley in the Dolomite Mountains offers great slopes and chic après-ski. The 140 km (87 miles) of piste attract both skiers and snowboarders. If you fancy a challenge, the Sella Ronda is a series of interconnected mountains; or try the slopes in the area of Tofana. An Olympic bobsled run may tempt the intrepid; otherwise head for the boutiques on Cortina's main street, Corsa Italia.
STAY: Cristallo Palace Hotel and Spa offers panoramic views of the valley. www.cristallo.it

MEGÈVE, FRANCE

Nestling at the foot of Mont Blanc, Megève is a scenic alpine town with upmarket shopping, great restaurants and casinos. Skiing is split between Mont d'Arbois, Rochebrune

and Le Jaillet, all of which are best suited to intermediates and beginners. Advanced skiers can head off-piste or try nearby Chamonix or Les Contamines. There's plenty here for the cross-country skier; runs are more tree-lined than usual, making it exceptionally beautiful. **STAY: the Chalet du Mont d'Arbois, a grand, beautifully set Swiss-style wooden chalet. www.chalet-montarbois.com**

MÉRIBEL, FRANCE
Nestled in the centre of Les Trois Vallées, this is the largest interlinked ski area in the world. With 600 km (370 miles) of slopes, it's great for intermediates and experts. Try the Ladies' Olympic downhill run, La Face, or the sweeping red runs of Mont Vallon. Snowboarders are well catered for and the off-piste opportunities are extensive. Ritzy Courchevel next door combines gentle cruising runs, as well as many expert challenges, with fabulous hotels, restaurants and shopping. **STAY: enjoy direct access to the pistes from Hotel Allodis. www.hotelallodis.com**

WINTER

"Winter kept us warm,
covering Earth
in forgetful snow…"

T.S. Eliot

Point-to-Point

A quintessentially British form of horse racing, the winter point-to-point season is a wonderful opportunity to explore some great locations, watch some exciting races, and soak up a uniquely equine ambience.

Point-to-point is also known as steeplechasing. It is named after a cross-country horse race first run in County Cork in 1752. Originally run between two churches – Buttervant and Doneraile – the riders would keep the steeples in their line of sight as they careered o'er hedge, wall and stream.

Point-to-point racing today is steeplechasing for amateur riders. Meetings are run locally by a hunt or recognised point-to-point club. Today, most races in the UK and Ireland are run over three miles (5 km). Some important races can be longer (the Lady Dudley Cup is three miles, two furlongs, and the Heythrop Men's Open is four miles [6.4 km]). Maiden events for younger horses are slightly shorter.

A three-mile race is generally two circuits of a course over a minimum of 18 fences. The fences are made of birch to a height of about 4 ft 6 in (1.3 metres). At least two fences should have ditches.

COURSES

There are usually over 200 fixtures per season. For a full listing of courses and event dates see www.pointtopoint.co.uk.

Bangor-on-Dee, North Wales
The majestic Pontcysyllte Aqueduct is not far from nearby Wrexham.

Barbury Castle Racecourse, Wiltshire
Visit nearby Barbury Castle or the prehistoric standing stones at Avebury.

Bishops Court, Devon
Visit Bishops Court in Exeter – a fine neo-Gothic country house, formerly the country palace of the Bishops of Exeter.

Charlton Horethorne, Somerset
Visit the old town of nearby Sherborne, famous for its medieval buildings, two castles, abbey and great antique shops.

Flete Park, Devon
Set in a natural amphitheatre in the Flete Park Estate on Dartmoor, there are some beautiful beaches nearby and sailing and surfing opportunities in the Estuary. Fishing (coarse, sea and game) is also good here.

Friars Haugh, Borders, Scotland
The rolling hills, moorlands and valleys of the Borders make for the ultimate horse country. There is a Festival of the Horse in May.

Hexham Racecourse, Northumberland
Visit Hadrian's Wall. Hexham itself is a delightful market town with a beautiful abbey.

Holnicote, Somerset
A picturesque course on the edge of Exmoor. Have lunch in Holnicote House and then take a stroll around the Estate.

Larkhill, Wiltshire
The course is situated on Salisbury Plain; a trip to nearby Stonehenge is a must.

Tweseldown, Hampshire
A famous old brick control tower, housing the commentators, dominates this course.

Hogmanay

Dating back to pagan celebrations of the Winter Solstice, the New Year's Eve festival of Hogmanay, enjoyed all over Scotland, is the perfect excuse for a party in Edinburgh.

The city parties like no other, with celebrations extending over four days. Technically, 31 December is Auld Year's Night and 1 January is Ne'erday, but celebrations start before and often carry on afterwards. Thankfully, 2 January is a welcome bank holiday in Scotland.

29 DECEMBER

TORCHLIGHT PROCESSION: join up with 20,000 torch-bearing vikings and revellers in a flaming procession from Parliament Square on the Royal Mile to Calton Hill. Enjoy the music of traditional pipes and drummers, and watch the ceremonial burning of the long-ship and wicker and willow effigies.

STAY
The gorgeous Prestonfield is the perfect antidote to excessive partying.
www.prestonfield.com

EAT
Take afternoon tea at The Balmoral. www.thebalmoralhotel.com
The Witchery By The Castle offers Gothic splendour. www.thewitchery.com
For a quick bite in town, the Vin Caffè Restaurant at Valvona and Crolla offers fantastic Italian cooking. www.valvonacrolla.co.uk

30 DECEMBER

NIGHT AFORE: kick off celebrations with a fabulous free street party on George Street, including processions, pipes and drums, ceilidh bands, street theatre and storytelling.

31 DECEMBER

THE HOGMANAY STREET PARTY: this is the main event, held in the city centre. You will need a free Street Party ticket to gain entry. In addition, Princes Street Gardens hosts a live music concert, and East Princes Street Gardens and Mound Square host the Ceilidh In The Gardens open air party. Both of these events require special tickets (they also include entry to the Street Party).

THE HOOG AND HOOG ROYALE: further dancing with ceilidhs and DJs can be enjoyed at The Assembly Rooms on George Street and The Queen's Hall on Clerk Street.

CANDLELIT CONCERT: for a more tranquil introduction to the New Year, try the evening Candlelit Concert in St Giles' Cathedral on the Royal Mile.

HOGMANAY FIREWORKS: at midnight, fireworks illuminate the hills around the city, and form a stunning backdrop to Edinburgh Castle. For those wishing to escape the crowds in the city centre, head to Calton Hill for a spectacular view.

1 JANUARY

THE LOONY DOOK: witness the brave and the bold throwing themselves into the icy waters of the Firth of Forth in South Queensferry. Fancy dress is optional.

ONE O'CLOCK RUN: after the previous night's festivities you may well just want to watch the fun run down the Royal Mile, with a glass of something restorative in hand.

Aviemore Sled Dog Rally

Wrap up warm and head for the forests around Aviemore to watch teams of dogs racing around Loch Morlich in the Cairngorms. This two-day event draws thousands of spectators each year.

The drivers of the dog teams ('mushers') travel from all over the country and the event attracts 200 teams annually. The race allows five breeds to enter: Siberian Huskies, Alaskan Malamutes, Samoyeds, Greenland Huskies, and Canadian Eskimo Dogs (many of the dogs also appear at Crufts). Every year, the competitors hope for snow but, if there's none, the race is run on three-wheeled bike-like rigs, rather than traditional sleds.

Teams of two to eight dogs reach speeds of approximately 20 mph as they dash along the four-mile (6.4-km) trail (a designated cross country ski course) around Loch Morlich in the Glenmore Forest Park. Some teams finish in less than 15 minutes.

If you fancy trying your hand as a musher, the Rothiemurchus Highland Estate, the UK's only sled dog centre, is nearby.

The Cairngorms also attract skiers and snowboarders. The funicular railway is a very graceful way to reach the top of the slopes.

Note: check local weather forecasts as the weather in the Cairngorms can be changeable. Driving conditions may become challenging on some of the higher mountain roads. www.rothiemurchus.net; www.cairngormmountain.org.uk

> "The more I see of man, the more I like dogs."
>
> Mme de Staël

STAY

Bunchrew House Hotel is a romantic 17th-century mansion on the shores of the Beauly Firth. Culloden House, set in 40 acres of parkland, was the headquarters of Bonnie Prince Charlie for the Battle of Culloden in 1746. www.bunchrew-inverness.co.uk; www.cullodenhouse.co.uk.

Dog Rally

Chinese New Year

London hosts the largest Chinese New Year celebrations outside Asia. With parades, performances and fireworks, this is one of the capital's most spectacular events.

Sometimes known as the Spring Festival, the date of Chinese New Year varies according to the lunar and solar calendars. Each new year is named after one of the 12 animals of the Chinese zodiac.

The celebrations begin in the late morning with a vibrant street parade along The Strand, before moving via Charing Cross to Shaftesbury Avenue and through Chinatown.

Trafalgar Square becomes the focus for the afternoon's events, featuring performances, dances and displays, often by visiting Chinese artists. For something more impromptu, head to Gerrard Street in Chinatown for food stalls and smaller parties.

STAY: pamper yourself in the luxurious spa at the Mandarin Oriental Hyde Park. www.mandarinoriental.com/london
EAT: enjoy authentic Cantonese food in the opulent, art deco surroundings of romantic China Tang at The Dorchester. www.chinatanglondon.co.uk

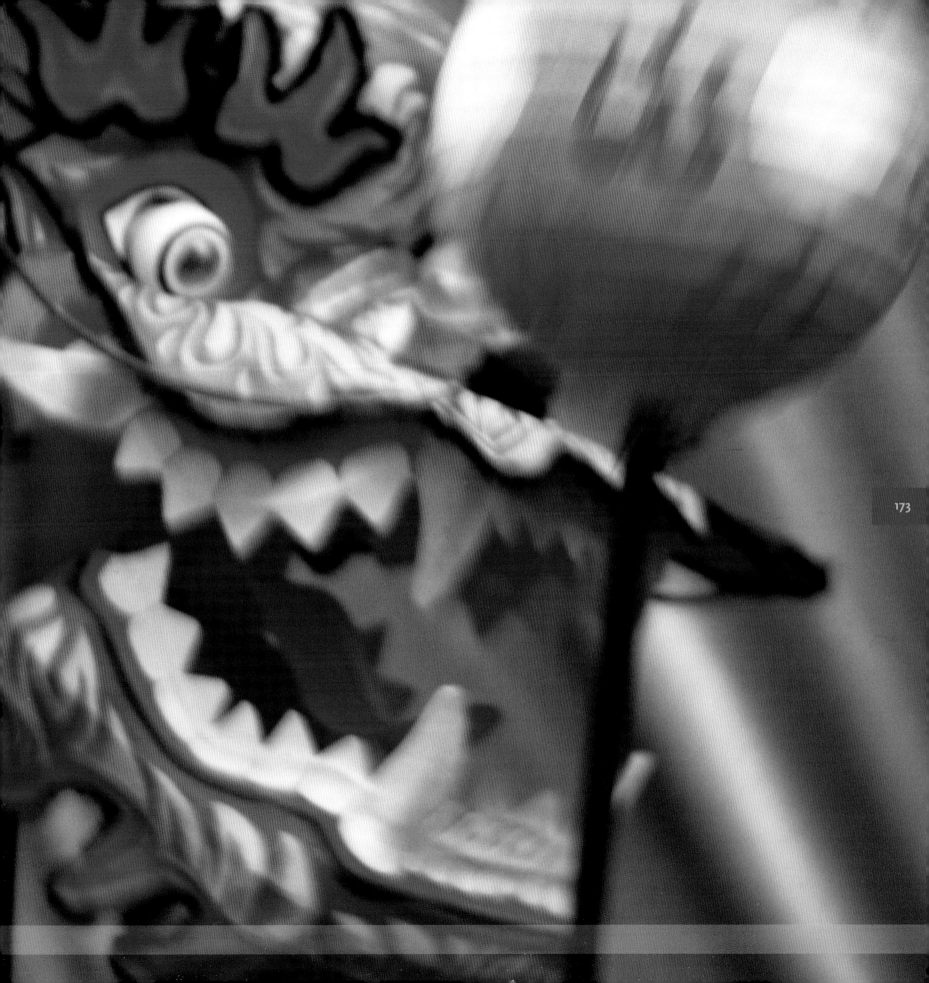

174

Six Nations

A mesmerising display of raw muscle power, the RBS Six Nations Championship is fought over seven winter weekends. The championship brings together the brutal drama of the pitch, enthusiastic and convivial spectators and six highly civilised European host cities.

The six competing nations are England, France, Scotland, Ireland, Wales and Italy. Each team plays the other five once, giving a total of 15 matches per Championship. The much coveted RBS Six Nations Championship Trophy is presented to the winning team on the final weekend; the wooden spoon for the losing team is purely figurative. The Championship is not only a chance to follow some great rugby, but an opportunity to meet fellow sporting enthusiasts and explore some uncharted regions.

VENUES

England: Twickenham, London

VISIT: the home of English rugby is perfectly situated for a drive around the historic sights of south-west London. Don't miss the neo-Palladian Chiswick House and the stunning Marble Hill House. Syon House, opposite Kew Gardens, is the last remaining ducal residence and country estate in Greater London.
STAY: The Bingham or The Gore.
www.thebingham.co.uk; www.gorehotel.com
EAT: La Trompette in Chiswick or Riva in Barnes. www.latrompette.co.uk

France: Stade de France, Saint-Denis, near Paris

VISIT: Basilique Saint-Denis, the burial site of many French monarchs. Then there is the whole of Paris at your feet...
STAY: Hôtel Costes, Hôtel de la Trémoille or the decadent Hotel du Petit Moulin.
www.hotelcostes.com; www.hotel-tremoille.com;
www.hotelpetitmoulinparis.com
EAT: indulge lavishly at Pâtisserie Pierre Hermé in Saint Germain des Prés. For great views, try Georges at the Pompidou Centre. For two Michelin-starred dining, visit L'Atelier de Joël Robuchon. www.centrepompidou.fr;
www.joel-robuchon.com

Ireland: Croke Park, Dublin

VISIT: celebrate a win in Temple Bar, snap up Dublin's finest fashions at Brown Thomas in Grafton Street, or stroll along Custom House Quay into Dublin Bay. If the city palls, you can take a spin through the Wicklow Mountains.
STAY: The Dylan or The Morgan for stylish boutique, or the Morrison Hotel for cool luxury. www.dylan.ie; www.themorgan.com;
www.morrisonhotel.ie
EAT: Thornton's in The Fitzwilliam Hotel or the two Michelin-starred Patrick Guilbaud.
www.fitzwilliamhotel.com/thorntons;
www.restaurantpatrickguilbaud.ie

Italy: Stadio Flaminio, Rome

VISIT: discover the gardens of Villa Celimontana on the Piazza della Navicella, or visit the Scala Santa (Holy Staircase) in San Giovanni.
STAY: Hassler Hotel, the central Hotel de Russie or the splendid Hotel Eden.
www.hotelhasslerroma.com;
www.hotelderussie.it;
www.starwoodhotels.com/lemeridien
EAT: L'Altro Mastai, or enjoy spectacular ice cream at Gelato Di San Crispino.
 www.laltromastai.it;
www.ilgelatodisancrispino.it

Scotland: Murrayfield, Edinburgh

VISIT: Edinburgh Castle is the obvious choice, but try a drive to Hopetoun House for some stately Georgian majesty. Admire the impressive collections of contemporary art at the Modern Art Galleries, set in extensive parkland that also serves as a sculpture park.
STAY: The Glasshouse or the ultra-funky Tigerlily. www.theetoncollection.com;
www.tigerlilyedinburgh.co.uk
EAT: the Michelin-starred Kitchin and Fourth Floor at Harvey Nichols offer breathtaking views of the city. www.thekitchin.com;
www.harveynichols.com

Wales: Millennium Stadium, Cardiff

VISIT: Cardiff Castle presides over the city and the recently regenerated Cardiff Bay offers some stunning architecture and cultural events. Drive inland to Cowbridge, in the Vale of Glamorgan. This historic town boasts 14th-century walls and a physic garden. Visit the nearby countryside village of St Hillary to see the impressive ruins of Beaupre Castle.
STAY: St David's Hotel or Jolyons.
www.stdavidshotel.com; www.jolyons.co.uk
EAT: Tides Grill in Saint David's, or great Thai at The Thai House. www.thaihouse.biz

St Valentine's Day

St Valentine, martyred on 14 February, has been honoured since the 5th century, when he became the patron saint of lovers. His saint's day is traditionally seen as an occasion for lovers to exchange cards and gifts. Respect this romantic tradition and treat your loved one to something really special.

DINNER

Heston Blumenthal's innovative 'molecular gastronomy' dishes put The Fat Duck firmly on the map. With a rare three Michelin stars, the restaurant's tasting menu is a unique experience. From snail porridge and parsnip cereal to the infamous egg and bacon ice cream, there is nowhere better to engage the senses. A dinner there will prove a memorable Valentine's Day experience. But be warned: bookings are usually taken two calendar months in advance.
www.fatduck.co.uk

ROMANCE

Tried and tested, nowhere is more romantic than Paris. For an exceptional experience, stay at the historic Hôtel de Crillon. Overlooking Place de la Concorde, this 18th-century palace is moments from the Champs-Elysées and some of the best Parisian sights. Dine at the hotel's renowned restaurant, Les Ambassadeurs. Critically acclaimed chef Jean Françoise-Piège creates some of the finest modern French cuisine, all in the perfect surroundings of the palace's former ballroom. www.crillon.com

OPERA

The sumptous Royal Opera House in London's Covent Garden is one of the world's leading opera houses. Enjoy some champagne before the performance and during the interval in the Paul Hamlyn Hall. This is the spectacularly restored Floral Hall, a beatiful glasshouse designed by E.M. Barry in 1858, which once formed part of the Covent Garden fruit and vegetable market. Stay at the nearby Covent Garden Hotel. The Four Poster Suite boasts a 10' x 10' bed.
info.royaloperahouse.org; www.firmdale.com

A WEEKEND IN NORFOLK

STAY: Cley Windmill. This famous landmark overlooks the salt marshes, offering a unique bed and breakfast experience.
www.cleymill.co.uk
VISIT: historic Holkham Hall is set in a Capability Brown landscaped deer park.
www.holkham.co.uk
WALK: walk out to Blakeney Point from Cley.

EAT: enjoy excellent local produce in relaxed surroundings at Fishes in Burnham Market. www.fishesrestaurant.co.uk
DRIVE: along the coast to Heacham, just past Hunstanton, to visit Norfolk Lavender. This is England's only lavender farm and hosts the national collection.
www.norfolk-lavender.co.uk

Vienna State Opera Ball

Opera Ball

"Dance till the stars
come down from the rafters.
Dance, dance, dance till you drop."

W.H. Auden

The Opera Ball, together with the New Year Concert,
is one of the highlights of the Viennese carnival season.

The annual Wiener Opernball takes place in the grand auditorium of the Vienna State Opera House on the Thursday preceding Ash Wednesday (which can be any time from 4 February to 10 March). This glamorous occasion, first inaugurated in 1854, has its roots in the dance evenings held in Vienna's aristocratic palaces during the late 18th century.

With its dazzling mix of ballet, polonaise and waltz, the Opera Ball is redolent of the grandeur of the Hapsburg Empire. It has become one of the biggest, most romantic middle-European society events of the year, attended by an eclectic array of aristocrats, bourgeoisie and bohemians.

WHAT TO EXPECT

Admission ticket price is €230 (book early). Boxes, tables and spectator tickets must be bought in addition to admission tickets.

Admission is from 9pm; the opening ceremony begins at 10pm with the entrance of the City's debutantes and their partners. The best vantage spot is from a box (from €8,500) as table views are limited (a table for two is approximately €160–€320). Spectator tickets are available from €85 per person for the gallery or €25 for a standing ticket.

Dancing opens with a formal polonaise, a showcase for Austrian high society, and socialising continues until 5am. Expect the romantic waltzes of Johann Strauss, Joseph Lanner and Carl Michael Ziehrer, as well as some swing and foxtrot. If formal dancing is beyond you, the Opera Ball Disco in the basement may be a better option.

Dress code: white tie (tails) for men. Long evening dresses or floor-length ball gowns for women.

STAY

Hotel Bristol is conveniently located opposite the State Opera House; Hotel Sacher is the home of Vienna's famous Sacher torte. www.starwoodhotels.com/luxury; www.sacher.com

EAT

Restaurant Steirereck in Vienna's Stadtpark is widely considered to be one of Austria's finest restaurants. www.steirereck.at

VISIT

Witness the classical horsemanship of the Lipizzan horse riding display at the Spanish Riding School. www.srs.at

SEE

The Leopold Museaum is home to an impressive collection of paintings by Egon Schiele and Gustav Klimt. Share Hundertwasser's utopian vision at Kunst Haus Wien. www.leopoldmuseum.org; www.hundertwasser.at

Venice Carnival

Join the masked revellers as one of the world's most beautiful cities scintillates with costumes, parties and processions. Held over the two weeks preceding Ash Wednesday, Carnival ends on Shrove Tuesday and begins two Fridays before.

Carnival dates back to 1268, but became famous as an essential stop on the Grand Tour in the 18th century. Banned by Mussolini in the 1930s, it was revived in 1979. The locals embrace the festivities and it is a major event in the Venetian calendar.

Synonymous with Carnival are the ornate masks, originally worn to conceal status within the hierarchical structure of Venetian society, and to aid anonymous flirting and gambling. Masks are still a must and are widely available. The *bauta*, often considered to be the most traditional mask, can cover the whole face, or just the top half, leaving the mouth free for eating and drinking.

Today, Carnival-goers are still addressed as 'Sior Maschera' (Signor Mask).

The Carnival is centred on Piazza San Marco, but parties, dances and street theatre will be encountered at every twist and turn in the city. Regular events are the Volo Dell'Angelo ('Flight of the Angel'), when confetti and balloons are showered from the top of the campanile onto the crowds gathered below in the loggia of the Doge's Palace. La Festa Delle Marie is a historical pageant, free for all to join, which starts in San Pietro di Castello. The Gran Corteo Storico and the mask procession – La Sfilata delle Maschere – are also not to be missed.

STAY
Luna Hotel Baglioni just behind Piazza San Marco or the iconic Hotel Cipriani.
www.baglionihotels.com;
www.hotelcipriani.com

EAT
Don't miss the seafood at Corte Sconta, a hidden gem located on Calle del Pestrin.

"Venice once was dear,
The pleasant place of all festivity,
The revel of the earth, the masque of Italy."

Lord Byron

Rye Bay
Scallop Festival

The picturesque East Sussex seaside town of
Rye hosts this ten-day festival every February
– its mouthwatering locally caught scallops
are said to be some of the best in the country.

> "There is no sincerer love than the love of food."
>
> George Bernard Shaw

Hotels and restaurants throughout the seaside town produce special menus featuring the famous local scallops. Cookery demonstrations, along with local award-winning wine tastings, are on offer during the festival.

Precipitous cobbled streets and a mere 5,000 inhabitants ensure that this medieval hill town maintains a village feel. The town became one of the strategically significant Cinque ports in 1189 and is steeped in history. Don't miss the Ypres Tower (pronounced 'wipers') and Lamb House, home of E.F. Benson. H.G. Wells, Henry James and Joseph Conrad are other famous Rye inhabitants.

STAY & EAT

The George, Rye's oldest coaching inn dating back to 1575, is a boutique hotel offering well-appointed rooms and a restaurant specialising in local, seasonal produce. Also try seasonal scallops at Webbe's at the Fish Café. www.thegeorgeinrye.com www.thefishcafe.com

VISIT

Don't miss neighbouring Winchelsea. Camber Sands, with its huge dunes, is a short drive away. Visit Sissinghurst Castle, home of author Vita Sackville-West, and Great Dixter House and Gardens, in Northiam, home of horticulturalist Christopher Lloyd. www.nationaltrust.org.uk/sissinghurst; www.greatdixter.co.uk

Indices

185

Chronological Index

187

Geographical Index

Drive *Index*

Events Index

Picture credits